Faithful in Christ Jesus

A Mission Reader

Urbana Advance

Preface by James McLeish
Compiled by Bill Goheen
with Karen Niedermayer

InterVarsity Press
Downers Grove
Illinois 60515

InterVarsity Press is the book-publishing division of Inter-Varsity Christian Fellowship, a student movement active on campus at hundreds of universities, colleges and schools of nursing. For information about local and regional activities, write IVCF, 233 Langdon St., Madison, WI 53703.

Biblical quotations, unless otherwise indicated, are from the Revised Standard Version of the Bible, copyrighted 1946, 1952, © 1971, 1973.

The map on page 82 is courtesy of Neighborhood Bible Studies, Inc.

ISBN 0-8308-1002-1

Library of Congress Catalog Card Number: 83-83227

Printed in the United States of America

17	16	15	14	13	12	11	10	9	8	7	6	5	4	3	2	1
98	97	96	95	94	93	92	91	90	89	88	87	86	85	84		

Inter-Varsity Christian Fellowship gratefully acknowledges the following
partners, all dedicated to spreading the gospel worldwide, whose grants made
the Urbana 84 advance reader possible:

The Broadhurst Foundation, in memory of William E. Broadhurst
The Henry Parsons Crowell and Susan Coleman Crowell Trust
The Walter Sewell family

Preface

It is great to know that you are interested in God's work in the world. By reading this book and studying it in depth, you will be able to decide more effectively on your place in God's world.

The prime purpose of this book is to prepare you to maximize your experience at the Inter-Varsity Christian Fellowship Student Missions Convention to be held the last five days of 1984 at the University of Illinois, Champaign-Urbana. It is commonly known as Urbana 84.

The closer I get to Urbana 84, the more conscious I become of the verse: "Be sober, be watchful. Your adversary the devil prowls around like a roaring lion, seeking some one to devour" (1 Pet 5:8).

The devil certainly does not want the church of Jesus Christ to declare his glory around the world. Therefore, you and I can fully expect him to oppose every effort we make as we prepare ourselves spiritually for Urbana 84.

We who participate in planning the convention, as well as the speakers, missionaries, students and others who will come to the convention, must utilize the full armor of God: truth, righteousness, the gospel of peace, and faith (Eph 6:14-16).

During these weeks before Urbana 84, ask God to help you ready yourself for your convention experience. This book will help. It is written in a practical manner so you can grow in your understanding of key ideas about world missions.

☐ What missions is all about
☐ Studies in Ephesians
☐ The practical side of preparing for Urbana 84
☐ Ideas on what you can do now about God's mission for you.

May I suggest you immerse yourself in this book and take seriously the questions it raises? You'll be surprised at what God will allow to happen in your life.

Another help would be to discuss this book as a group. At the end are questions for ten group discussions, including the four Bible studies. If you and a few friends are going to Urbana or are just thinking about missions, get together and work your way through these discussions. Your time together can be stimulating and profitable.

It is my prayer that God will add his richest blessing as you serve him throughout the world.

For his sake,
James McLeish
President and Chief Executive Officer
Inter-Varsity Christian Fellowship, U.S.A.

Prolog:
Inter-Varsity Christian
Fellowship and Urbana

The Urbana missions convention is sponsored by the Inter-Varsity Christian Fellowships of the United States and Canada. It's primary purpose is to glorify Christ by helping students find God's place for them in world missions and thus to serve the church in strengthening its ministry. But Inter-Varsity is much more than Urbana.

Inter-Varsity Is Students

Inter-Varsity is students declaring God's glory on campuses, students living out their faith in Jesus Christ, students united by and rooted in Scripture, students reaching cross-culturally with the gospel.

Inter-Varsity is not a church, it is not a denomination, and it is not a mission board. *Inter-Varsity is part of the church as students and faculty from many denominations in hundreds of student-run campus fellowships commit themselves to follow Christ as Lord.*

What is this fellowship like? Each local "chapter" of IVCF strives to follow Jesus Christ in different ways. Many get together daily to praise God and to pray. In weekly Bible studies they dig into the Word for themselves. Students and faculty also encourage each other to share Christ with non-Christian friends. One faculty member shared Christ in his classes, and this encouraged students to share their faith. A dozen came to Christ as a result.

Inter-Varsity Is Training

But students and faculty are not alone. As a national movement IVCF provides many resources for campus Christians. Take, for example, one of the most important: Inter-Varsity staff members visit campuses to teach from the Scripture, to train in evangelism, to give an example of what it means to follow Christ daily. At one university, a staff member led a discipleship training program for a core of students; from this students started an evangelistic Bible study and began personal evangelism; as a result, a new believer enrolled in the freshman discipleship course held soon after. The spiritual "cycle of life" continues.

Inter-Varsity students are also involved in training camps and conferences. The annual Fort Lauderdale Beach Evangelism Project at Easter, Bible and Life study weekends, and the crosscultural Student Training in Missions program are just a few of many.

Various branches of IVCF offer still other resources. The Student Missions Fellowship (SMF) works to present overseas missions at Christian schools. The Nurses Christian Fellowship (NCF) shares the same goals as IVCF as it seeks to help nursing school students and graduates bring Christ into their nursing care. The TWENTYONEHUNDRED team produces multimedia shows for use on campus.

Committed discipleship is encouraged through literature. Inter-Varsity Press and HIS magazine both aim to help the mind grow under Christ's lordship.

Inter-Varsity Is Worldwide Fellowship

Inter-Varsity in Canada and the United States are only two member movements of the worldwide International Fellowship of Evangelical Students (IFES). The movement in Brazil distributes Portuguese literature through bookstores, schools and newsstands in that country and in Portugal. In Nigeria, Christian students recently confronted classmates and others at the International Black Arts Festival with the lordship of Jesus Christ in contrast to the occult. Schloss Mittersill, a castle in the Austrian Alps, bursts at the seams with the international family gathering for training conferences, Bible seminars, and evangelistic houseparties. These are only a few of the many activities of the over 50 national movements joined together in student outreach.

Inter-Varsity Is People

Inter-Varsity is more than Urbana—people on campus and off, salaried and volunteer, from across North America, many churches; people behind the scenes, typing, keeping records, writing, planning, in national, regional and area offices; men and women entrusted with the corporate and legal responsibilities on the corporations and boards of IVCF-USA and IVCF-Canada; business people and homemakers serving on Local Committees to raise the funds needed to support the campus work—all these and more help make up Inter-Varsity.

A Glossary on Missions

Animism—the primitive belief that animals, natural forces (rain, thunder) and inanimate objects possess personal souls often having supernatural powers.

Call—a strong conviction that God wants a person to serve him in some specific way and/or place. This does not usually come through some exotic experience but through prayerful investigation of the possibilities for mission.

Church Growth—a movement within modern missions concerned with multiplication of converts and congregations.

Church planting—the process of beginning local Christian congregations generally in areas where the gospel has not been previously received.

Contextualization—understanding and communicating biblical truth in such a manner that hearers perceive it to be relevant in their culture.

Crosscultural communication—the way people of one society convey ideas to those of another society who differ in such areas as language, values, thought forms and behavior.

Crosscultural evangelism—communicating the good news of Jesus Christ across cultural barriers. Ralph Winter has coined the terms *E-1 Evangelism* (evangelism to non-Christians who have the same culture), *E-2 Evangelism* (evangelism that is crosscultural but able to build on certain overlapping areas, like French and Spanish cultures) and *E-3 Evangelism* (evangelism from one culture to a totally different one) to further clarify the task of crosscultural evangelism.

Culture—the integrated system of learned patterns of behavior, ideas and products characteristic of a society.

Culture shock—the experience of a person who is entering a society very different from the one to which he or she is accustomed. It is sometimes characterized by confusion, physical illness, insecurity, fear of defensiveness.

Deputation—the activity/ministry of missionaries or missionary appointees through which they establish a relationship with sending churches and individuals for prayer and financial support.

Discipling—building up believers and training them to witness to others.

Evangelism—communicating to others the good news of salvation through Jesus Christ.

Expatriate—a person who lives in a country not his or her own.

Faith mission—a mission agency which is not related to a denomination, receiving its personnel and support from denominational and/or unaffilated groups.

Furlough—a period during which the missionary returns to his sending country to gain new perspective, improve skills and renew contact with supporters.

Hinduism—a worldwide religion predominant in India which is characterized by belief in reincarnation and one supreme deity which exists in many forms and natures.

Holistic—emphasizing the needs of the whole person (spiritual, physical, intellectual, social and emotional).

House churches—small groups of Christians, usually with nonprofessional leaders, who meet together as congregations in an individual's house or apartment.

Indigenous church—a church which reflects the culture in which it is located, administering and supporting its own life and outreach.

Islam—the religious faith of Muslims based on the belief that Allah is the sole diety and Muhammad is his prophet.

Liberation theology—a movement in the modern church which emphasizes the need to free men from oppressive economic and social structures, often Marxist in orientation.

Mission agency—an organization which furthers crosscultural evangelism and the establishing of new churches by planning strategy for evangelizing some part or parts of the world and recruiting, training and sending missionaries. A *home mission* agency focuses on non-Christians within the country of the agency.

Missionary—a supported worker who is involved in the expansion of the church in a culture other than his or her own. *Career missionaries* (also called professional missionaries) are individuals choosing long-term missionary service. *Short-term missionaries* are individuals involved in missionary service for two years or less. *Summer missionaries* do not join a mission agency but serve as volunteers for three to six months with the purpose of learning about missions firsthand while giving all the assistance they can.

Missions—the activities of a sending church through which it seeks to communicate the gospel across cultural boundaries with a view to establishing churches that will evangelize.

Moratorium on missions—a proposal debated within the church suggesting that all missionaries return to their sending countries in order to allow each nation to thoroughly indigenize its Christian activities. Decisions would be made later by each country about how many missionaries, if any, should return to it.

Nationalization—to convert (a section of industry, agriculture, commerce or the church) from foreign control and ownership to control and ownership by those in the country itself.

Nationals—a more appropriate term than *natives* for the people of another country. *Native* connotes being uncivilized.

Nonprofessional missionaries—(also called *vocational witnesses*) individuals who support themselves in secular, salaried positions abroad with the primary purposes of evangelizing, discipling and planting churches.

Paternalism—treating people in a fatherly or condescending manner; for example, a mission might continue an authority role which inhibits the maturing of the church it has established.

Pioneer evangelism—taking the gospel to areas which have never heard the gospel.

Saturation evangelism—a strategy which involves mobilizing the whole church to concentrate on making Christ known in a given area.

Short-termers—individuals involved in missionary service for two years or less.

Syncretism—the attempt to combine differing religious or philosophical beliefs.

Theological Education by Extension (TEE)—individualized training in the Bible and church-related skills, provided for church leaders where they live and minister.

Third World—nations, especially in Africa, Latin America and Asia, not aligned with communist or capitalist countries. Also called *developing nations*.

Tribalism—a greater loyalty for one's own tribe than for one's country or religion.

Universalism—the belief that all people in the world will eventually be forgiven and be received by God; sometimes referred to as being "implicit" or "anonymous" Christians.

Unreached/unevangelized people—a homogenous group of people among which there is no indigenous community of believing Christians with adequate numbers to evangelize this people group without outside (crosscultural) assistance.

Western nations (or the West)—those countries which are largely influenced by European or American culture.

World-class city—a city of international significance with a population of at least one million.

Part I

Looking at World Missions in the Eighties

Ideas about missions that you will find fascinating and enlightening.

John Kyle *focuses our attention on the sunrise of missions efforts in the eighties.*

David Bryant *alerts us to the crucial need for prayer.*

John R. W. Stott *summarizes God's promise to Abraham and helps us to see a biblical perspective on missions.*

Ralph D. Winter *helps us understand the task before us.*

Isabelo Magalit *urges Americans to seek three essential qualifications before becoming missionaries.*

Gordon MacDonald *celebrates the church as a beginning and end of our mission.*

Raymond J. Bakke *graphically illustrates the need for new strategies to reach the cities of the world.*

1

Overseas Missions Projections for the 1980s

John E. Kyle

Never in my lifetime have I seen such a keen interest in world missions among American college students than during this decade. In the face of this phenomenon there has never been another time in the history of world missions when the recruitment of new overseas missionaries was so strategic for reaching the 3.0 billion unreached peoples of our earth.

In the past three years alone some forty-five thousand young people on both sides of the Atlantic have demonstrated a concern for seeking out their place in world missions at the Urbana 79 and 81 Conferences and at the Mission 80 and 83 Congresses held in Lausanne, Switzerland.

What does all this interest in world missions among young adults and students mean? What will be the consequences of this growing interest during the 1980s? I believe that God has been preparing a great harvest worldwide and that he is in the process of preparing great numbers of laborers to be thrust out into his harvest from the Western nations.

Will the existing mission sending agencies be able to handle an increased number of candidates, or will new agencies as well as strategies for reaching the lost need to be developed? Most people feel that existing agencies are going to be stretched, and that we will see the simultaneous creation of new agencies and new strategies.

Missions strategists are thinking bigger today than ever before, having pinpointed the areas of greatest need. The world's 3.0 billion unreached people have been identified as the Chinese, Hindu, Muslim and tribal peoples, comprising some 16,750 unreached people groups. The definition of unreached peoples helps to pinpoint the target: A people group among which there is no indigenous community of believing Christians with adequate numbers and resources to evangelize this people group without outside (cross-cultural) assistance.

Along with the increased interest in world missions among Western young people, there has been a parallel interest and burden in developing nations. We are, therefore, beginning to see the emergence of international missionary teams. This may well be the trend of the future as more mission agencies become truly international and not merely Western.

Many thoughtful people are beginning to question whether the churches of North America will be able to financially support the growing missionary force from North America. God in his sovereignty is raising up new forces to assist the local church to rise to this challenge. For example, the Association of Church Missions Committees (ACMC), founded in 1971, is assisting over five hundred churches in reorganizing their mission programs.

There will continue to be a great need for career planning and counseling of college students to help connect them with the right mission sending agency, receive the right training and finally get overseas as a missionary.

There is no question that world missions over the past one hundred years has been greatly blessed by God. The sun never sets on the church of Jesus Christ. We are not in the sunset of missions.

Rather, we are actually living in the *sunrise of missions*. This decade could prove to be the most exciting in which to live in all the 1983 years of Christian history.

We need to pray to the Lord of the harvest as never before for revival and renewal of the church in North America so that thousands of missionaries will be quickly sent out to reach the three billion who yet await the gospel of Jesus Christ. This is why Inter-Varsity Missions is so committed to promoting "concerts of prayer" across our planet as described by David Bryant in the following article. There is no more strategic need today than that of unified prayer.

John Kyle has been a businessman, pastor, missionary and missions executive. He is currently serving as the missions director of Inter-Varsity Christian Fellowship—U.S.A., and director of Urbana 84.

2

Concerts of Prayer: Waking Up for a New Missions Thrust

David Bryant

As I have talked with many people about missions, I have observed two types of responses to missions. One is an openness toward missions—even an innocence—that is the most encouraging we have seen for a decade at least. But the other is a paralysis of faith.

This paralysis is understandable. The *immensity* and the *complexity* of the task are enough to stun anyone. There are billions to be reached and thousands of culture groups to be penetrated. Likewise, the *uncertainties* of the task are immobilizing. There are so many risks to face and so many options to choose from in over seven hundred Protestant mission agencies, not to mention numerous Catholic orders.

One observation of the causes of paralysis is the *invisibleness of corporate prayer*. Prayer is our one major recourse for vitality and spiritual vigor. As I travel, I discover congregations and student groups fermenting exciting ideas and projects, laying dynamic plans, expanding programs and facilities. But I don't see a united ministry of intercession.

Another observation is that we suffer from a *poverty of models:* we see so few who evidence unselfish obedience to a clearly integrated vision; who do so in a quiet, relentless movement of prayer; and who, as a result, bring the rest of us with them.

My point is that a new missions thrust may fail to emerge, not because God's people are unwilling, but because we are *unable* to perform it. Even among churches which show positive reactions to the more creative approaches in missions thinking, there is the tendency to keep missions at arms length, as little more than a "hobby" (albeit, far more meaningful than some have known it to be for a long time). Many still seem unable to make the crucial leap from missions-as-an-interest to missions-as-a-cause.

The great barrier we face in world evangelization is not an external one of culture or nationalism, but the internal paralysis of our faith.

What can set us free? What can raise us up? The answer seems obvious. We need a new work from God. We need renewal, revival, awakening.

What is awakening? It is when the Spirit enlivens the church with new pulsations of vision and faith. Awakening comes as God gives us new eyes to see the gospel all over again or to see dimensions of that gospel that have become fuzzy. Often this means waking up not only to what Christ has done for and in us but, beyond that, to what he wants to do *through* us. Awakening is God reintroducing us to Jesus. We come to see him in new ways. That leads us to trust him in new ways. That leads us to love and obey him in new ways. That leads us to move with him in new ways to fulfill his global cause. We are alerted to the full implications of Christ's lordship. It has to lead, ultimately, to a new missions thrust.

How did God's redemptive mission become the longest sustained human endeavor of all time? How did the church come to be eighty-three million times larger than when it began? How is it that the gospel has directly or indirectly altered for good the life of most of the nations on earth? One undeniable trend can be seen throughout: consistently, there have been pioneers of faith banded together in movements of prayer. Sometimes these movements have been called concerts of prayer.

There is a threefold development in God's pattern of awakening: first, there are prayer movements, then there is revitalization, then expansion. In every case, the starting point is what I call "pioneering" faith. In the past, such pioneers were God's gift to the body of Christ. We must have them again. We need to pray for them to emerge and be willing to become one ourselves if we are to see a new missions thrust.

Pioneers of faith aren't necessarily more spiritual than other Christians, but they are more full of faith than many. Facing the immensity, complexity and uncertainty of the task, they don't boast all the answers, but they do boast in knowing God.

To use another expression, we need *pacesetters* of God's promises, who will believe all he wants to do through his people. Such pacesetters sense a God-given mandate to lead out in faith so that others can see their model and follow. Prayer is their hallmark. They are a humble cadre of seekers who spearhead renewed momentum for missions by a faith that grows through united prayer.

Basically, pioneers of faith are models. They exhibit the kind of faith that compels us to pursue purposes bigger than ourselves. Surely God wants to give us such models. We need them if we are to see billions reached for Christ. Even more, I believe the church in North America is longing for such models. I think we may be rounding a corner where we will search less for spiritual celebrities to mirror experience and look more for models to mirror excellence in faith.

As J. Edwin Orr documents in *Campus Aflame*, during the past three hundred years it has been students, more often than not, who have served the church as models, pioneers and pacesetters. And I believe God is preparing such people today. He is calling them to pick up the torch of faith from such historical student missions thrusts and to bring it to the forefront of what God does in our generation.

Pioneers of faith are needed, wanted, and they are emerging. But how are they to mobilize for maximum impact in their pioneering ministry for the body of Christ? Any new missions thrust must begin and grow through aggressive intercession. Like a battalion, pioneers of faith must first band together to set the pace—primarily through intercession.

Such a movement of prayer will retain five key characteristics. First, it will be marked by a *visible union*. C. H. Fahs comments, "Student missionary uprisings, like college revivals, when traced to their sources, are shown to have started invariably in a group of students associated for prayer" (quoted by J. Edwin Orr, *Campus Aflame* [Regal Press, 1971], p. 120).

Second, a movement of prayer will also be marked by *solidarity*. Here we tell God, based on the great sweeps of his purposes in Scripture: "I want what you want." We align our will and desires with his.

Third, it will be characterized by *advocacy*. As advocates we tell God, based on the great longings of the church and the world: "They need what you have promised."

Fourth, there will be *pursuit*. We pursue God in prayer, based on the utter unacceptableness of things as they stand. We tell him: "This must become all you intend it to be."

Finally, concerts of prayer will be marked by the two great biblical sweeps of God's heart: the *revival of God's people* and the *advancement of his kingdom* throughout the nations.

Extraordinary prayer is not determined so much by how long we pray or how often, but rather that we do pray, that we do so "in concert" and that we pray for those things which God has clearly shown us he is ready and wanting to do.

In any prayer movement, dynamic tension must always be maintained between church renewal and world evangelization. Each thrives on the other and drives us to the other, if kept in proper balance. Renewal prevents burnout in the task of missions. And missions keeps us from letting the fruits of renewal dry up. If we maintain this tension, the ministry of intercession will be our most effective step in pioneering faith for Christ's global cause.

I often find two kinds of prayer groups going on in churches and campuses, usually unaware of each other. Some are praying for revival. Others are praying for missions. If we could get both groups together and integrate their individual agendas, we would have a most explosive mix! I call these two great agendas *fullness* and *fulfillment*. We need to seek the fullness of Christ in his global church for the fulfillment of his global cause.

Let me conclude by suggesting several items of prayer under the two great agendas:

Fullness (Revival, Awakening)

☐ Pray for God to raise up *prayer bands* of world Christians on our campuses, in our churches and in our mission agencies.

☐ Ask for new awareness of God's *holiness*. The church needs to be holy as he is holy if we are to have significant impact for his glory in the world.

☐ Pray for a fresh sense of God's *love* for the world and a rekindling of our love for him. We need to be filled with Christ's love.

☐ Pray for *reconciliation*, so that Christians may become transparent before him and each other and, in repentance and forgiveness, band together for the cause of Christ.

☐ Ask God to renew our *world vision* and *faith* to move forward into the challenge of reaching the nations.

☐ Pray that the church would awaken to Christ's universal *authority*, the basis of her commitment to the world missionary movement.

☐ Pray for *gratitude* for all that God has already done for us individually and collectively, so we will delight to bring what we have found to those who have never heard.

☐ Pray for a sense of *accountability* to Christ to share our lives with the billions locked in extreme spiritual and physical poverty, so we will repent of hoarding the gospel and release its full impact of love and justice worldwide.

☐ Pray that God would fire commitments to Christ's global cause among the hundreds of thousands of Christian *students* worldwide and prepare them to assume leadership and sacrifice to carry out that commitment.

Fulfillment (Advancement, Missions)

☐ Pray that God will be *glorified* throughout the earth, among all peoples everywhere. Tell him what it will mean to you personally when he is glorified.

☐ Pray for an intentional, sacrificial penetration of major human barriers worldwide, that churches may be planted within every people group within this generation. (This will provide God's kingdom with a base of operation in each group.)

☐ Pray for spiritual hunger among Muslims, Chinese, Hindus, Buddhists. Ask that those who have yet to hear may find a new sense of God's reality and an awakened desire to seek him.

☐ Ask that Satan may be bound and routed, that Christ's victory on the cross would break Satan's hold on nations and cultures.

☐ Pray for world leaders and governments and for the outcome of world events. (All of these can directly affect the free course of the gospel within a nation or within a people group.)

☐ Pray for major global issues which impinge upon a breakthrough of the gospel and are a part of the moral darkness that must be penetrated. Such issues include global hunger, nuclear proliferation, political and economic repression.

☐ Pray for God's people everywhere to see those near by them whose ways of living differ from them significantly enough to cut them off from a normal witness of the gospel—to see them and to reach them.

☐ Ask God to give the church the gift of apostles (those who are "sent out"—1 Cor 12:28, 21). We need hundreds of thousands of new crosscultural messengers, missionaries and tentmakers, to be sent out by the churches around the world. Ask God to give the church wisdom to know who these people are, to set them apart for the work to which he has called them and to send them forth by a movement of prayer and sacrifice.

☐ Pray for specific missionaries. Pray for those you know personally and those you learn about in other ways, including some of the over fifteen thousand out of Third World churches. Pray for those working among a particular people group that you also desire to see reached.

☐ Pray for those peoples and places where the doors are open for hundreds of more laborers to enter.

☐ Ask God to raise up a movement of senders worldwide—people who know for certain that God has called them to send out a new force of crosscultural witnesses, and who embrace their assignment with the same vision and sacrifice as they ask of those who go.

David Bryant serves nationally as Missions Specialist with IVCF. An author and speaker, Bryant travels worldwide, teaching and preaching on the subject of prayer and the world mission of the church. He is currently a member of the National Prayer Committee.

3

The Living God
Is a Missionary God

John R. W. Stott

Millions of people in today's world are extremely
hostile to the Christian missionary enterprise. They regard it as
politically disruptive (because it loosens the cement which binds
the national culture) and religiously narrow-minded (because it
makes exclusive claims for Jesus), while those who are involved in
it are thought to suffer from a kind of arrogant imperialism. And
the attempt to convert people to Christ is rejected as an unpardon-
able interference in their private lives. "My religion is my own
affair," they say, "Mind your own business, and leave me alone to
mind mine."

It is essential, therefore, for Christians to understand the
grounds on which the Christian mission rests. Only then shall we
be able to persevere in the missionary task, with courage and
humility, in spite of the world's misunderstanding and opposition.

More precisely, biblical Christians need biblical incentives. For we believe the Bible to be the revelation of God and of his will. So we ask: Has he revealed in Scripture that "mission" is his will for his people? Only then shall we be satisfied. For then it becomes a matter of obeying God, whatever others may think or say. Here we shall focus on the Old Testament, though the entire Bible is rich in evidence for the missionary purpose of God.

The Call of Abraham

Our story begins about four thousand years ago with a man called Abraham, or more accurately, Abram as he was called at that time. Here is the account of God's call to Abraham.

Now the LORD said to Abram, "Go from your country and your kindred and your father's house to the land that I will show you. And I will make of you a great nation, and I will bless you, and make your name great, so that you will be a blessing. I will bless those who bless you, and him who curses you I will curse; and by you all the families of the earth shall bless themselves." So Abram went, as the LORD had told him; and Lot went with him. Abram was seventy-five years old when he departed from Haran. (Gen. 12:1-4)

God made a promise (a composite promise, as we shall see) to Abraham. And an understanding of that promise is indispensable to an understanding of the Bible and of the Christian mission. These are perhaps the most unifying verses in the Bible; the whole of God's purpose is encapsulated here.

By way of introduction we shall need to consider the setting of God's promise, the context in which it came to be given. Then we shall divide the rest of our study into two. First, *the promise* (exactly what it was that God said he would do) and second—at greater length—*its fulfillment* (how God has kept and will keep his promise). We start, however, with the setting.

Genesis 12 begins: "Now the LORD said to Abram." It sounds abrupt for an opening of a new chapter. We are prompted to ask: "Who is this 'LORD' who spoke to Abram?" and "Who is this 'Abram' to whom he spoke?" They are not introduced into the text out of the blue. A great deal lies behind these words. They are a key which opens up the whole of Scripture. The previous eleven chapters lead up to them; the rest of the Bible follows and fulfills them.

What, then, is the background to this text? It is this. "The LORD" who chose and called Abram is the same Lord who in the beginning created the heavens and the earth, and who climaxed his creative work by making man and woman unique creatures in his own likeness. In other words, we should never allow ourselves to forget that the Bible begins with the universe, not with the planet earth; then with the earth, not with Palestine; then with Adam the father of the human race, not with Abraham the father of the chosen race. Since, then, God is the Creator of the universe, the earth and all mankind, we must never demote him to the status of a tribal deity or petty godling like Chemosh the god of the Moabites, or Milcom (or Molech) the god of the Ammonites, or Baal the male deity, or Ashtoreth the female deity, of. the Canaanites. Nor must we suppose that God chose Abraham and his descendants because he had lost interest in other peoples or given them up. Election is not a synonym for elitism. On the contrary, as we shall soon see, God chose one man and his family in order, through them, to bless *all* the families of the earth.

We are bound, therefore, to be deeply offended when Christianity is relegated to one chapter in a book on the world's religions as if it were one option among many, or when people speak of "the Christian God" as if there were others! No, there is only one living and true God, who has revealed himself fully and finally in his only Son Jesus Christ. Monotheism lies at the basis of mission. As Paul wrote to Timothy, "There is one God, and there is one mediator between God and men, the man Christ Jesus" (1 Tim. 2:5).

The Genesis record moves on from the creation of all things by the one God and of human beings in his likeness, to our rebellion against our own Creator and to God's judgment upon his rebel creatures—a judgment which is relieved, however, by his first gospel promise that one day the woman's seed would "bruise," indeed crush, the serpent's head (3:15).

The following eight chapters (Gen. 4—11) describe the devastating results of the Fall in terms of the progressive alienation of human beings from God and from our fellow human beings. This was the setting in which God's call and promise came to Abraham. All around was moral deterioration, darkness and dispersal. Society was steadily disintegrating. Yet God the Creator did not abandon the human beings he had made in his own likeness (Gen. 9:6). Out of the prevailing godlessness he called one man and his family, and promised to bless not only them but through them the whole world. The scattering would not proceed unchecked; a grand process of ingathering would now begin.

The Promise
What then was the promise which God made to Abraham? It was a composite promise consisting of several parts.

First, it was the promise of *a posterity*. He was to go from his kindred and his father's house, and in exchange for the loss of his family God would make of him "a great nation." Later in order to indicate this, God changed his name from "Abram" ("exalted father") to "Abraham" ("father of a multitude") because, he said to him, "I have made you the father of a multitude of nations" (17:5).

Second, it was the promise of *a land*. God's call seems to have come to him in two stages, first in Ur of the Chaldees while his father was still alive (11:31; 15:7) and then in Haran after his father had died (11:32; 12:1). At all events he was to leave his own land, and in return God would show him another country.

Third, it was the promise of *a blessing*. Five times the words *bless* and *blessing* occur in 12:2-3. The blessing God promised Abraham would spill over upon all mankind.

A posterity, a land and a blessing. Each of these promises is elaborated in the chapters that follow Abraham's call.

First, *the land*. After Abraham had generously allowed his nephew Lot to choose where he wanted to settle (he selected the fertile Jordan valley), God said to Abraham: "Lift up your eyes, and look from the place where you are, northward and southward and eastward and westward; for all the land which you see I will give to you and to your descendants for ever" (13:14-15).

30

Second, *the posterity.* A bit later God gave Abraham another visual aid, telling him to look now not to the earth but to the sky. On a clear, dark night he took him outside his tent and said to him, "Look toward heaven and number the stars." What a ludicrous command! Perhaps Abraham started, "1, 2, 3, 5, 10, 20, 30 . . . ," but he must soon have given up. It was an impossible task. Then God said to him: "So shall your descendants be." And we read: "He believed the Lord." Although he was probably by now in his eighties, and although he and Sarah were still childless, he yet believed God's promise and God "reckoned it to him as righteousness." That is, because he trusted God, God accepted him as righteous in his sight.

Third, *the blessing.* "I will bless you." Already God has accepted Abraham as righteous or (to borrow the New Testament expression) has "justified him by faith." No greater blessing is conceivable. It is the foundation blessing of the covenant of grace, which a few years later God went on to elaborate to Abraham: "I will establish my covenant between me and you and your descendants after you . . . for an everlasting covenant, to be God to you and to your descendants after you . . . and I will be their God" (17:7-8). And he gave them circumcision as the outward and visible sign of his gracious covenant or pledge to be their God. It is the first time in Scripture that we hear the covenant formula which is repeated many times later: "I will be their God and they shall be my people."

A land, a posterity, a blessing. "But what has all that to do with mission?" you may be asking with impatience. My answer is "Everything! Be patient a little longer and you will see." Let us turn now from the promise to the fulfillment.

The Fulfillment
The whole question of the fulfillment of Old Testament prophecy is a difficult one in which there is often misunderstanding and not a little disagreement. Of particular importance is the principle, with which I think all of us will agree, that the New Testament writers themselves understood Old Testament prophecy to have not a *single* but usually a *triple* fulfillment—past, present and future. The

31

past fulfillment was an immediate or historical fulfillment in the life of the nation of Israel. The present is an intermediate or gospel fulfillment in Christ and his church. The future will be an ultimate or eschatological fulfillment in the new heaven and the new earth.

God's promise to Abraham received an immediate, historical fulfillment in his physical descendants, the people of Israel.

God's promise to Abraham of a numerous, indeed of an innumerable, posterity was confirmed to his son Isaac (26:4, "as the stars of heaven") and his grandson Jacob (32:12, "as the sand of the sea"). Gradually the promise began to come literally true. Perhaps we could pick out some of the stages in this development.

The first concerns the years of slavery in Egypt, of which it is written, "The descendants of Israel were fruitful and increased greatly; they multiplied and grew exceedingly strong; so that the land was filled with them" (Ex. 1:7; cf. Acts 7:17). The next stage I will mention came several hundred years later when King Solomon called Israel "a great people, that cannot be numbered or counted for multitude" (1 Kings 3:8). A third stage was some three hundred fifty years after Solomon; Jeremiah warned Israel of impending judgment and captivity, and then added this divine promise of restoration: "As the host of heaven cannot be numbered and the sands of the sea cannot be measured, so I will multiply the descendants of David my servant" (33:22).

So much for Abraham's posterity; what about the land? Again we note with worship and gratitude God's faithfulness to his promise. For it was in remembrance of his promise to Abraham, Isaac and Jacob that he first rescued his people from their Egyptian slavery and gave them the territory which came on that account to be called "the promised land" (Ex. 2:24; 3:6; 32:13), and then restored them to it some seven hundred years later after their captivity in Babylon. Nevertheless, neither Abraham nor his physical descendants fully inherited the land. As Hebrews 11 puts it, they "died in faith, *not* having received what was promised." Instead, as "strangers and exiles on the earth" they "looked forward to the city which has foundations, whose builder and maker is God" (see Heb. 11:8-16, 39-40).

God kept his promises about the posterity and the land, at least in part. Now what about the blessing? Well, at Sinai God confirmed and clarified his covenant with Abraham, and pledged himself to be Israel's God (for example, Ex. 19:3-6). And throughout the rest of the Old Testament God went on blessing the obedient while the disobedient fell under his judgment.

Perhaps the most dramatic example comes at the beginning of Hosea's prophecy, in which Hosea is told to give his three children names which describe God's awful and progressive judgment on Israel. His firstborn (a boy) he called "Jezreel," meaning "God will scatter." Next came a daughter "Lo-ruhamah," meaning "not pitied," for God said he would no longer pity or forgive his people. Lastly he had another son "Lo-ammi," meaning "not my people," for God said they were not now his people. What terrible names for the chosen people of God! They sound like a devastating contradiction of God's eternal promise to Abraham.

But God does not stop there. For beyond the coming judgment there would be a restoration, which is described in words which once more echo the promise to Abraham: "Yet the number of the people of Israel shall be like the sand of the sea, which can be neither measured nor numbered" (Hos. 1:10). And then the judgments implicit in the names of Hosea's children would be reversed. There would be a gathering instead of a scattering ("Jezreel" is ambiguous and can imply either), "not pitied" would be pitied, and "not my people" would become "sons of the living God" (1:10—2:1).

The wonderful thing is that the apostles Paul and Peter both quote these verses from Hosea. They see their fulfillment not just in a further multiplication of Israel but in the inclusion of the Gentiles in the community of Jesus: "Once you were no people but now you are God's people; once you had not received mercy but now you have received mercy" (1 Pet. 2:10; cf. Rom. 9:25-26).

This New Testament perspective is essential as we read the Old Testament prophecies. For what we miss in the Old Testament is any clear explanation of just *how* God's promised blessing would overflow from Abraham and his descendants to "all families of the earth." Although Israel is described as "a light to lighten the nations," and has a mission to "bring forth justice to the nations" (Is. 42:1-4, 6; 49:6), we do not actually see this happening. It is only in the Lord Jesus himself that these prophecies are fulfilled, for only in his day are the nations actually included in the redeemed community. To this we now turn.

God's promise to Abraham receives an intermediate or gospel fulfillment in Christ and his church.

Almost the first word of the whole New Testament is the word *Abraham.* For Matthew's Gospel begins: "The book of the genealogy of Jesus Christ, the son of David, the son of Abraham. Abraham was the father of Isaac. . . ." So it is right back to Abraham that Matthew traces the beginning not just of the genealogy but of the gospel of Jesus Christ. He knows that what he is recording is the fulfillment of God's ancient promises to Abraham some two thousand years previously. (See also Lk. 1:45-55, 67-75.)

Yet from the start Matthew recognizes that it isn't just *physical* descent from Abraham which qualifies people to inherit the promises, but a kind of *spiritual* descent, namely, repentance and faith in the coming Messiah. This was John the Baptist's message to crowds who flocked to hear him: "Do not presume to say to yourselves, 'We have Abraham as our father'; for I tell you, God is able from these stones to raise up children to Abraham" (Mt. 3:9; Lk. 3:8; cf. Jn. 8:33-40). The implications of his words would have shocked his hearers since "it was the current belief that no descendant of Abraham could be lost" (J. Jeremias, *Jesus' Promise to the Nations,* SCM Press, 1958, p. 48).

And God has raised up children to Abraham, if not from stones, then from an equally unlikely source, namely, the Gentiles! So Matthew, although the most Jewish of all four Gospel writers, later records Jesus as having said, "I tell you, many will come from east and west and sit at table with Abraham, Isaac, and Jacob in the kingdom of heaven, while the sons of the kingdom will be thrown into the outer darkness" (8:11-12; cf. Lk. 13:28-29).

It is hard for us to grasp how shocking, how completely topsy-turvy, these words would have sounded to the Jewish hearers of John the Baptist and Jesus. *They* were the descendants of

34

Abraham; so *they* had a title to the promises which God made to Abraham. Who then were these outsiders who were to share in the promises, even apparently usurp them, while they themselves would be disqualified? They were indignant. They had quite forgotten that part of God's covenant with Abraham promised an overspill of blessing to *all* the nations of the earth. Now the Jews had to learn that it was in relation to Jesus the Messiah, who was himself seed of Abraham, that all the nations would be blessed.

The apostle Peter seems at least to have begun to grasp this in his second sermon, just after Pentecost. In it he addressed a Jewish crowd with the words: "You are the sons . . . of the covenant which God gave to your fathers, saying to Abraham, 'And in your posterity shall all the families of the earth be blessed.' God, having raised up his servant [Jesus], sent him to you first, to bless you in turning every one of you from your wickedness" (Acts 3:25-26). It is a very notable statement because he interprets the blessing in the moral terms of repentance and righteousness and because, if Jesus was sent "first" to the Jews he was presumably sent next to the Gentiles, whose "families of the earth" had been "far off" (cf. Acts 2:39) but were now to share in the blessing.

It was given to the apostle Paul, however, to bring this wonderful theme to its full development. For he was called and appointed to be the apostle to the Gentiles, and to him was revealed God's eternal but hitherto secret purpose to make Jews and the Gentiles "fellow heirs, members of the same body, and partakers of the promise in Christ Jesus through the gospel" (Eph. 3:6).

Negatively, Paul declares with great boldness, "Not all who are descended from Israel belong to Israel, and not all are children of Abraham because they are his descendants" (Rom. 9:6-7).

Who then are the true descendants of Abraham, the true beneficiaries of God's promises to him? Paul does not leave us in any doubt. They are believers in Christ of whatever race. In Romans 4 he points out that Abraham not only received justification by faith but also received this blessing *before he had been circumcised.* Therefore Abraham is the father of all those who, whether circumcised or uncircumcised (that is, Jews or Gentiles), "follow the example of [his] faith" (Rom. 4:9-12). If we "share the faith of Abraham," then "he is the father of us all, as it is written, 'I have made you the father of many nations' " (vv. 16-17). Thus neither physical descent from Abraham, nor physical circumcision as a Jew, makes a person a true child of Abraham, but rather faith. Abraham's real descendants are believers in Jesus Christ, whether racially they happen to be Jews or Gentiles.

What then is the "land" which Abraham's descendants inherit? The letter to the Hebrews refers to a "rest" which God's people enter now by faith (Heb. 3—4). And in a most remarkable expression Paul refers to "the promise to Abraham and his descendants, that they should *inherit the world*" (Rom. 4:13). One can only assume he means the same thing as when to the Corinthians he writes that in Christ "all things are yours, whether Paul or Apollos or Cephas or the world or life or death or the present or the future, all are yours" (1 Cor. 3:21-23). Christians by God's wonderful grace are joint heirs with Christ of the universe.

Somewhat similar teaching, both about the nature of the promised blessing and about its beneficiaries, is given by Paul in Galatians 3. He first repeats how Abraham was justified by faith, and then continues: "So you see that it is men of faith who are the sons of Abraham" and who therefore "are blessed with Abraham who had faith" (vv. 6-9). What then is the blessing with which all the nations were to be blessed (v. 8)? In a word, it is the blessing of salvation. We were under the curse of the law, but Christ has redeemed us from it by becoming a curse in our place, in order "that in Christ Jesus the blessing of Abraham might come upon the Gentiles, that we might receive the promise of the Spirit through faith" (vv. 10-14). Christ bore our curse that we might inherit Abraham's blessing, the blessing of justification (v. 8) and of the indwelling Holy Spirit (v. 14). Paul sums it up in the last verse of the chapter (v. 29): "If you are Christ's, then you are Abraham's offspring, heirs according to promise."

But we have not quite finished yet. There is a third stage of fulfillment still to come. *God's promise to Abraham will receive an ultimate or eschatological fulfillment in the final destiny of all the redeemed.*

36

In the book of Revelation there is one more reference to God's promise to Abraham (7:9ff). John sees in a vision "a great multitude which no man could number." It is an international throng, drawn "from every nation, from all tribes and peoples and tongues." And they are "standing before the throne," the symbol of God's kingly reign. That is, his kingdom has finally come, and they are enjoying all the blessings of his gracious rule. He shelters them with his presence. Their wilderness days of hunger, thirst and scorching heat are over. They have entered the promised land at last, described now not as "a land flowing with milk and honey" but as a land irrigated from "springs of living water" which never dry up. But how did they come to inherit these blessings? Partly because they have "come out of the great tribulation" (evidently a reference to the Christian life with all its trials and sufferings), but mostly because "they have washed their robes and made them white in the blood of the Lamb," that is, they have been cleansed from sin and clothed with righteousness through the merits of the death of Jesus Christ alone. "*Therefore* are they before the throne of God."

Speaking personally, I find it extremely moving to glimpse this final fulfillment in a future eternity of that ancient promise of God to Abraham. All the essential elements of the promise may be detected. For here are the spiritual descendants of Abraham, a "great multitude which no man could number," as countless as the sand on the seashore and as the stars in the night sky. Here too are "all the families of the earth" being blessed, for the numberless multitude is composed of people from every nation. Here also is the promised land, namely, all the rich blessings which flow from God's gracious rule. And here above all is Jesus Christ, the seed of Abraham, who shed his blood for our redemption and who bestows his blessings on all those who call on him to be saved.

Conclusion

Let me try to summarize what we learn about God from his promise to Abraham and its fulfillment.

First, he is the God of history. History is not a random flow of events. For God is working out in time a plan which he conceived in a past eternity and will consummate in a future eternity. In this historical process Jesus Christ as the seed of Abraham is the key figure. Let's rejoice that if we are Christ's disciples we are Abraham's descendants. We belong to his spiritual lineage. If we have received the blessings of justification by faith, acceptance with God, and of the indwelling Spirit, then we are beneficiaries today of a promise made to Abraham four thousand years ago.

Second, he is the God of the covenant. That is, God is gracious enough to make promises, and he always keeps the promise he makes. He is a God of steadfast love and faithfulness. Mind you, he does not always fulfill his promises immediately. Abraham and Sarah "died in faith, *not* having received what was promised, but having seen it and greeted it from afar" (Heb. 11:13). That is, although Isaac was born to them in fulfillment of the promise, their seed was not yet numerous, nor was the land given to them, nor were the nations blessed. All God's promises come true, but they are inherited "through faith *and patience*" (Heb. 6:12). We have to be content to wait for God's time.

Third, he is the God of blessing. "I will bless you," he said to Abraham (Gen. 12:2). "God ... sent him [Jesus] to you first, to bless you," echoed Peter (Acts 3:26). God's attitude to his people is positive, constructive, enriching. Judgment is his "strange work" (Is. 28:21). His principal and characteristic work is to bless people with salvation.

Fourth, he is the God of mercy. I have always derived much comfort from the statement of Rev. 7:9 that the company of the redeemed in heaven will be "a great multitude which no man could number." I do not profess to know how this can be, since Christians have always seemed to be a rather small minority. But Scripture states it for our comfort. Although no biblical Christian can be a universalist (believing that all mankind will ultimately be saved), since Scripture teaches the awful reality and eternity of hell, yet a biblical Christian can—even must—assert that the redeemed will somehow be an international throng so immense as to be countless. For God's promise is going to be fulfilled, and Abraham's seed is going to be as innumerable as the dust of the earth, the stars of the sky and the sand on the seashore.

Fifth, he is the God of mission. The nations are not gathered in automatically. If God has promised to bless "all the families of the earth," he has promised to do so "through Abraham's seed" (Gen. 12:3; 22:18). Now *we* are Abraham's seed by faith, and the earth's families will be blessed only if *we* go to them with the gospel. That is God's plain purpose.

I pray that these words, "all the families of the earth," may be written on our hearts. It is this expression more than any other which reveals the living God of the Bible to be a missionary God. It is this expression too which condemns all our petty parochialism and narrow nationalism, our racial pride (whether white or black), our condescending paternalism and arrogant imperialism. How dare we adopt a hostile or scornful or even indifferent attitude to any person of another color or culture if our God is the God of "all the families of the earth"? We need to become global Christians with a global vision, for we have a global God.

So may God help us never to forget his four-thousand-year-old promise to Abraham: "By you and your descendants *all* the nations of the earth shall be blessed."

John R. W. Stott has a worldwide ministry as a Bible expositor and writer. The best known of his many books is Basic Christianity. *He is currently director of the London Institute. This article was condensed from a talk given at the Urbana 76 missions convention which appeared in* Declare His Glory among the Nations. *© 1977 by Inter-Varsity Christian Fellowship of the U.S.A.*

4

The Need in World Mission Today

Ralph D. Winter

As we prepare to confront the future of world mission, before we do anything else, we must sum up our progress to the present. This leads us to an awesome awareness of the task as yet unfinished, that is, the need.

At the International Congress on World Evangelization at Lausanne, I gave an address, the central thesis of which can be summed up in a single sentence: *while there are 3.0 billion people who do not even call themselves Christians, over three-quarters of them are beyond the range of any kind of normal (cultural-near-neighbor) evangelization by existing churches.*

By "normal evangelism" I do not mean what is normally now being done; I refer to all of those various kinds of evangelism which believers in presently existing congregations *would be capable of launching* without surmounting unusual barriers of language and social structure. This has also been called cultural-near-neighbor evangelism or monocultural evangelization or E-0 or E-1 evangelism. E-0 evangelism is winning *nominal Christians* to Christ, and E-1 evangelism is winning people *who do not call themselves Christians* but who are in the same cultural sphere as the church. These surely must continue and must be vastly expanded.

But even assuming a great spiritual evangelizing revival were to sweep every existing congregation in the world, those congregations reaching out in normal evangelism would still be stopped short by cultural barriers before reaching three-fourths of the non-Christians in the world today: *from that point on,* crosscultural, E-2 (evangelism that is crosscultural but able to build on certain overlaps, like French and Spanish cultures) and E-3 (evangelism from one culture to a totally different one) would be necessary.

The Three Major Blocs

Figure 1 is a fairly exact scale drawing (as are all the figures in this article, adapted from the table on p. 52) representing the largest racial and cultural bloc of humanity—the Chinese. The large circle on the right represents those Chinese who do not consider themselves Christians. The small circle to the left represents the number of Chinese who do consider themselves Christians. The circle

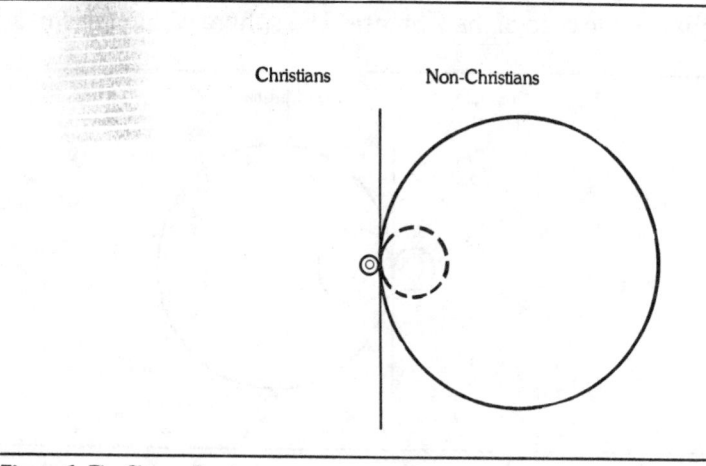

Christians   Non-Christians

Figure 1. The Chinese People

within the left-hand circle represents an estimate of the number of truly committed Chinese Christians by whom I do not mean, for example, all who call themselves evangelicals, but rather truly committed believers, specifically *those Christians on whom we may count to help finish the task.*

The first impression this diagram of the Chinese gives us is the vastness of the unfinished task. But a startling second message comes through when we note that the dotted circle within the large right-hand circle represents the limited number of Chinese whom even crosscultural evangelists are able to reach during this present epoch of history; that is, the dotted circle represents the 38 million Chinese outside mainland China. But even if China were open, there is in Chinese society an amazing mosaic of subcultural barriers which would put most Chinese beyond the reach of normal evangelism as we have defined it.

Another large bloc of non-Christians is the Hindu. In Figure 2 the large circle again represents non-Christians, this time the number of Hindus who do not consider themselves Christians. Note that here, as in the case of the Chinese, I am referring to a culturally, not a racially or a religiously, defined group. Thus we may say that the left-hand circle represents the number of people of Hindu cultural background who consider themselves Christians. Note carefully that this Christian circle is proportionately larger than in the case of the Chinese. The sphere within the small

Christians   Non-Christians

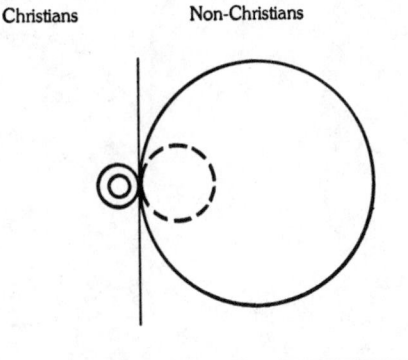

Figure 2. The Hindu People

circle (the committed Christians) is larger too, yet it is smaller relative to the total number of Christians; that is, there are more nominal Christians of Hindu background both absolutely and relatively.

Once more, if we are sensitive at all to the heart of God, we must be stunned and crushed by the vastness of the unreached populations within this major bloc of mankind. But the second message is again more shocking: it is the stubborn fact not often recognized that only a relatively small number of people in India are reachable by normal evangelistic efforts on the part of even the Christians in India. These reachable people, represented by the dotted circle, are the Harijans—the remaining non-Christian peoples in the formerly "untouchable" category.

Let me repeat that by *normal* I do not mean what is now normally being done. A reliable—but staggering—report indicates that 98% of all current evangelistic efforts in India, whether missionary or national, are not even focused on non-Christians, but (as is true in the United States) are attempts of *believing* Christians to reach *nominal* Christians and bring them back into the vital fellowship of the church. In terms of the figure, it is Christians of the inner sphere reaching nominal Christians in the doughnut-shaped space around them. These are specifically *not* efforts to reach even the people in the dotted circle, the non-Christians of Hindu culture *who are culturally approachable* by Christians, people with the same cultural traditions—shall we say *caste?*

On the one hand, then, Christians in India are not (with only rare exceptions) even *attempting* to win totally non-Christian people. But on the other hand, if the Christians of India did suddenly and strenuously reach out to every last person within their various cultural traditions, they would not even in that hypothetical case be able to win anyone outside of the dotted circle unless, note, *unless* they made new beachheads by the utilization of what would substantially be traditional missionary techniques (involving the establishment of the kind of professional agencies capable of crossing serious cultural barriers).

All countries have their caste systems. Sometimes the barriers are linguistic differences, economic differences or other types of cultural differences. The barriers of this type are almost always socially describable. They are not spiritual barriers. While the spiritual barriers are the same whether a nominal Christian becomes committed to Christ or a total non-Christian becomes committed to Christ, the cultural barriers, where they exist, are always a stubborn technical problem *in addition.*

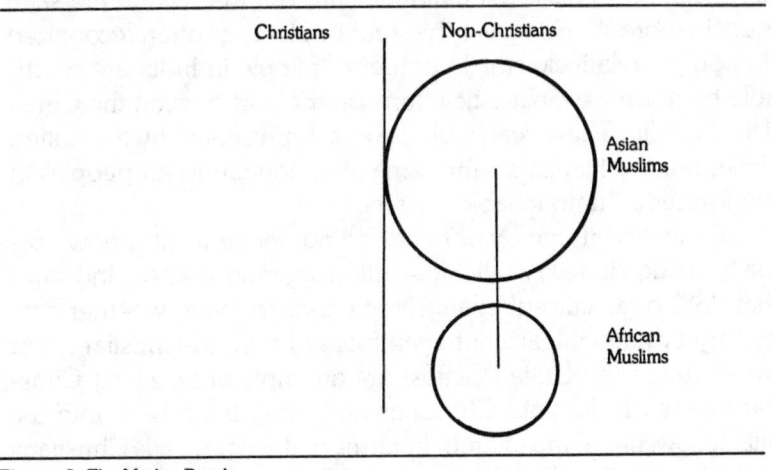

Figure 3. The Muslim People

The third large non-Christian cultural tradition is pictured in Figure 3. Since there are huge numbers of Muslims both in Africa and Asia, we have used two circles to depict the non-Christians of Muslim cultural background. In this case a curious and tragic fact appears: there are not enough Christians of Muslim extraction that we can even depict them in a small circle as we did for the Chinese and the Hindus.

Up to now in mission history we have either not *known* how or have not been *able* to achieve the development of a "Muslims for Jesus" movement anywhere, with one or two possible exceptions. While we have from ten to thirty thousand Christians of Jewish heritage in the United States, despite the fact that they were brought up from infancy to react against the name of Jesus Christ, the amazing fact is that Muslims are brought up to revere Jesus highly. Their holy book, the Koran, technical scholars today point out, actually elevates Jesus above Mohammed. But to date there are very few Muslims for Jesus.

We have now seen three major blocs of non-Christians, and in each case only a tiny proportion of the people in these blocs represent people whose social groupings would allow them easily to become part of (and also attract their friends to) any existing congregation of believers in Christ. To sum up, normal evangelism, even if effectively and fully launched from all present congregations, is totally inadequate to grapple with this major part of the unfinished task.

The Remaining World

Now, once we have recognized the existence of these three major groups, the remaining, or "other" non-Christians in Asia represent (by contrast) only a mopping-up operation. The astonishing novelty in Figure 4 is the large number of Christians culturally related to the remaining non-Christians. The number of Christians is of a totally different magnitude and proportion than in the previous diagrams.

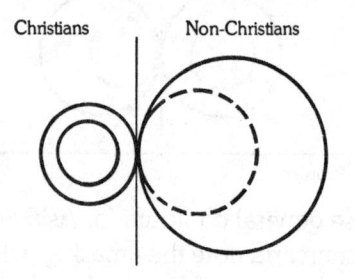

Christians   Non-Christians

Figure 4. Other Asian Peoples

Who are the peoples in this catch-all group of "other" non-Christian Asians? There are, for example, 100 million Japanese. Are they all reachable by normal evangelism? Lest we exaggerate the number requiring crosscultural evangelism, let us recall that while there are some fairly momentous cultural barriers to be crossed in the winning of all Japanese into the present variety of Japanese churches, such cultural barriers are in no way comparable to the barriers that prevent normal evangelism from even

45

touching the vast bulk of the Hindus or the Muslims.

Thus the dotted circle—people who can (even conceivably) be reached by normal evangelism—is very much larger and includes not only many Japanese but also many Buddhists for whom there are in fact viable Christian traditions nearby that do not present a major social obstacle to their affiliation. In this estimate we are certainly not *over*- but *underestimating* the proportions of those who cannot be reached by normal (E-0 or E-1) evangelism.

Let us now move on to the last bloc of non-Christians outside of the Western world. We have already mentioned the non-Christian Muslims of Africa. This diagram shows the Africans who are neither Christian nor Muslim. Recalling that Africa was only 3% Christian in 1900, we stand amazed and pleased that the number of Christians is nearly equal to the number of non-Christians who are not Muslims! The number of committed Christians is large too.

Christians Non-Christians

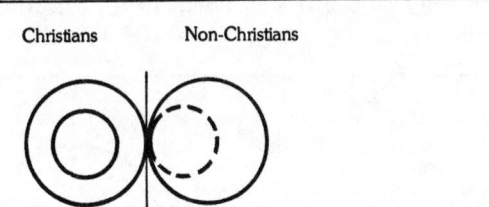

Figure 5. Other African Peoples

In view of these general contours for Asia and Africa, let us put them in a single chart and note the amazingly different proportions in the Western world. Figure 6 breaks the Western world down by isolating the population of the United States. Since these circles are drawn on the same scale as before, we see immediately that the Western world contains most of the nominal Christians. We can verify by eye that 85% of the nominal Christians are in the West while only a little over half of the committed Christians are in the West. It is even more obvious that the ratio of Christians to non-Christians is radically different in the Western world when compared to every area of Asia and Africa except non-Muslim Africa. Here then are the hard facts that maintain the credence of that long useful adage that where there are ten men at one end of a log and only one at the other, the priorities are obvious, especially if the ten men are at the smaller end of the log.

The Blunt Truth

To fully digest these diagrams can rightly absorb hours and hours of deep thought and earnest prayer. Here in scale drawing is the primary need in missionary strategy in the world today. Let us stop to recognize the following: (1) the great bulk of people on this planet are concentrated in Africa and Asia; (2) an even greater proportion of Africa and Asia (than the Western world) consists of peoples who do not consider themselves Christian; (3) the three largest cultural blocs of mankind—the Chinese, Hindus and Muslims—have only tiny Christian communities, if any at all, related to them; (4) in the case of China and India, only a very small proportion of the non-Christians are within normal evangelistic striking range of the existing Christians; and (5) despite the small number of Christians from within these large cultural traditions, their efforts to evangelize are mainly soaked up by the spiritual needs of the nominal belt that surrounds them.

Once we size up the need in these terms, it must be clear that *the only effective answer to the major part of this need can come from specialized crosscultural organizations of the type represented by a standard mission society, either local or foreign.*

Since dealing with nominal Christians is the kind of evangelism most American Christians are acquainted with, it is not surprising that Americans who become involved in traditional foreign missions generally have a tough time figuring out how to do crosscultural evangelism, and even if they do figure it out, have an even tougher time explaining to people back home how different pioneer missionary work is from the normal evangelism of cultural near-neighbors.

In these words I have no desire whatsoever to belittle the immensity of the commonly understood task of bringing about spiritual renewal among lifeless nominal Christians. This task of renewal is not only big, it is truly urgent, because worldwide outreach to non-Christians is considerably blunted by the scandalous behavior of nominal Christians back home in the Western world.

But the blunt truth is that if you had to guess at the proportion of all the evangelizing energies of evangelicals around the world expended on the renewing of nominal Christians you would probably come up with something like 97%. Yet, nominal Christians, though numerous, are only about one-fourth as numerous as the total of nominal Christians and non-Christians. Why should

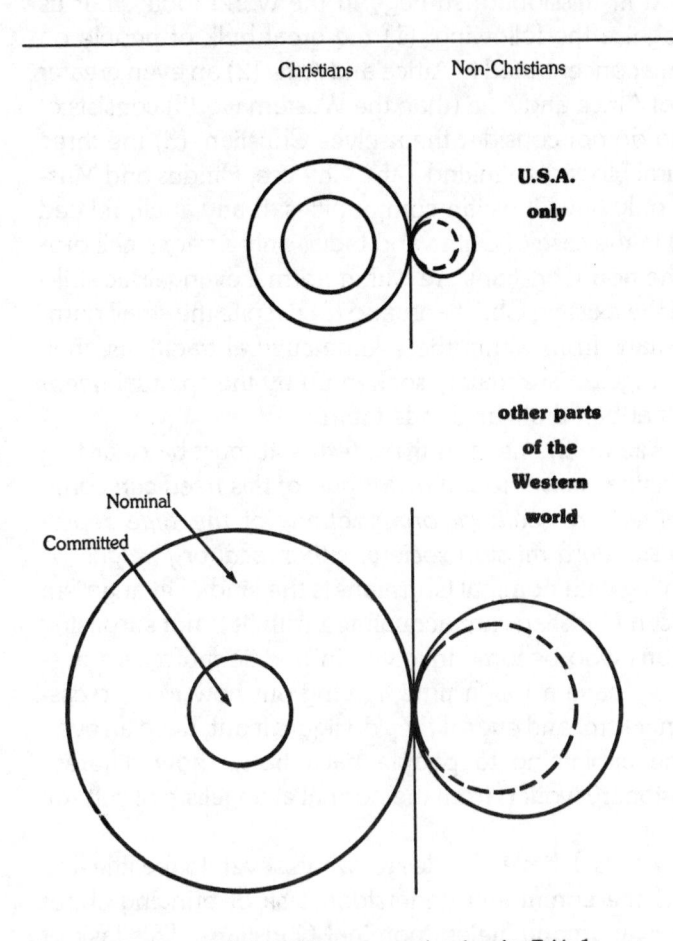

Numerical data from which these drawings are made is found in Table 1.

Figure 6. Western World (Europe, Russia, Americas, Australia, New Zealand)

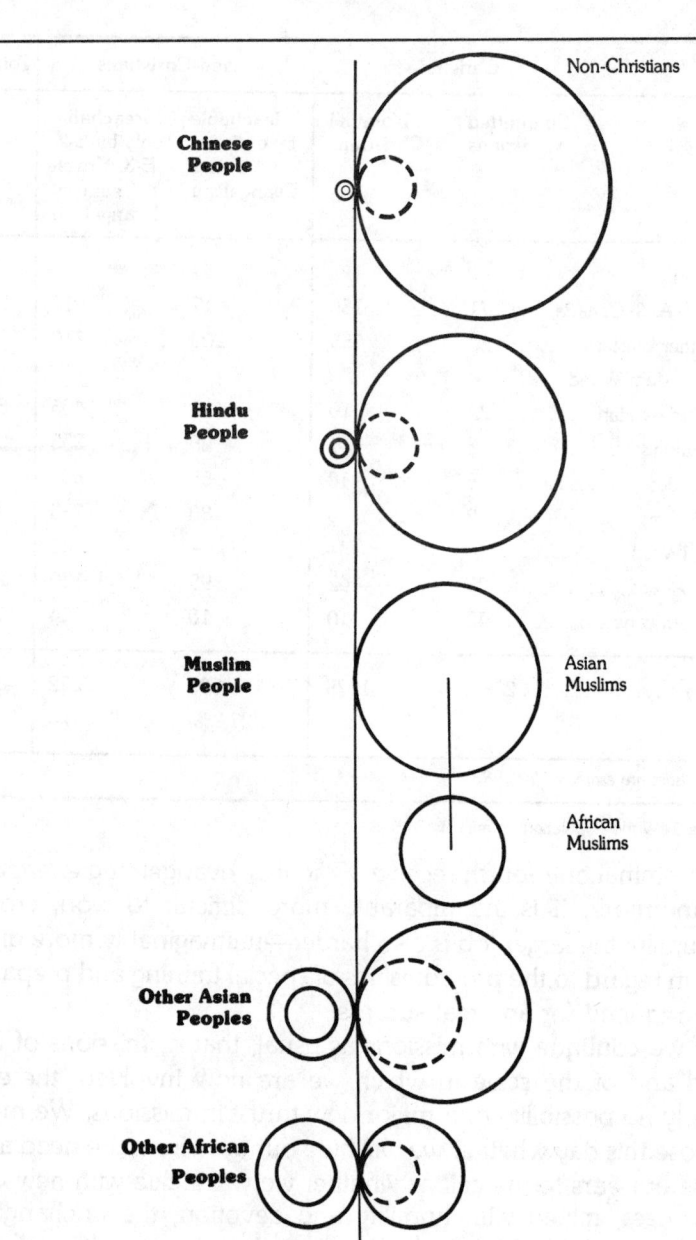

Figure 7. Non-Western World (Asia, Africa)

	Christians		Non-Christians		Totals
	Committed Christians	Nominal Christians	Reachable by ordinary E-1 Evangelism	Reachable only by E-2, E-3, Cross-cultural Evangelism	
Western					
U.S.A. & Canada	71	150	17	12	250
Other Western	70	755	200	110	1135
Non-Western World					
Chinese Han	22	10	400	405	837
Buddhist	2	1	25	255	283
Hindus	8	10	55	537	610
Muslims	.2	0	30	733	763
(West)	–	–	–	26	26
Other Asians	25	42	95	120	282
Other Africans	40	110	10	24	184
Totals	238.2	1078	832 (27.2%)	2222 (72.8%)	4370

All statistics are estimates for 1982

Table 1. World Population (in millions)

the nominal one-fourth receive 97% of all evangelizing energies? Furthermore, it is incomparably more difficult to work cross-culturally: the larger job is also harder—unimaginably more difficult in regard to the prerequisities of special training and preparation required for any real success.

If we continue with missions as usual, that is, missions of the kind and of the scale in which we are now involved, there is simply no possibility of a major new thrust in missions. We must choose this day whether we will hide our eyes from the need and close our ears to the call or whether we will tackle with new decisiveness, mixed with humility and devotion, the unchanging command of a faithful God whose searching heart is still seeking. To hold back now will lead to misery, guilt and failure; the other choice leads through new open doors into the most spectacular mission challenge that any generation in human history has ever faced. If we will awake to new, daring obedience, the future is as bright as the promises of God.

Ralph D. Winter (Ph.D., Cornell) is the director of the United States Center for World Missions. This article is reprinted from The Grounds for a New Thrust in World Mission *by Ralph D. Winter (1977) by permission of the William Carey Library, P.O. Box 128-C, Pasadena, CA 91104.* © *1977 by the Evangelical Foreign Missions Association. Statistics were added in 1982 and revised in 1983.*

5

The Messenger's Qualifications

Isabelo Magalit

I was at Urbana 76. It was a most moving moment, when the call to commitment was made, to see half of the 17,000 people in this auditorium stand up, signifying their commitment to actively seek God's will concerning world evangelization.

"But the famous Urbana Convention is a joke!" said a veteran Western missionary to me shortly after I returned to Manila. "We have deceived these young people," he continued. "Where will these thousands of missionaries go? Where can they go? Who will accept them? When will Western, particularly North American, mission agencies wake up to the fact that their missionaries are simply not welcome in many parts of the world?"

Is my missionary friend, who is an American, right? Is the day of the Western missionary coming to an end? Is it time to say good-bye to the great Urbana missionary conventions? Should the burden of making the gospel known to the ends of the earth now be shifted to the younger churches of the Third World?

No, definitely no. World evangelism is the responsibility of the whole church, no less of the older churches of Europe and America than of the younger churches of Asia, Africa and Latin America. And no more the responsibility of the one group than of the other. In fact, the dimensions of world evangelism are so awesome that only the whole church throughout the world, working in proper partnership, can get the task done. How to work together, as full partners, *that* is the question. It is a question that deserves plenty of attention, not the least in a missions convention such as Urbana. But no, the day of missions from the West is not over.

The time has certainly come for Western-based missions to give more careful consideration to the kind of missionaries they send. Of course missionaries from elsewhere need the same qualifications. Korean missionaries working in Bangkok need the same qualifications as American missionaries in Manila. But the precise outworking of the qualifications will differ somewhat. Today, I come to you as a Filipino—a brother in Christ—speaking to North Americans who are eager to proclaim the Lord Jesus to all nations.

You must face up to the significance of your distinction— especially you who are Americans—that you come from the world's mightiest nation, which has implications for the missionary enterprise launched from your shores. The drama in Teheran does not detract from the greatness of your power. It illustrates it. The seizure of the U.S. embassy by Iranian students is an act of desperation—the wild swing of a little boy against what he regards as a bully. Yes, your political power has implications.

Your presence and your influence, your interests and your policies, your opinions and your goods—for example, Coke and Superman—are so ubiquitous around the globe that your missionaries cannot help being visible, easily identified as American.

You can affirm that identity unequivocally, without apology, sincerely believing that it stands for what is best in the world. Like one of your television preachers, you may even be convinced that "God loves America above all nations." Yes, you can proudly affirm your American identity.

Or, you can repudiate it in a valiant effort to make sharp the difference between American culture and the eternal gospel. We have all been sensitized to this issue of gospel and culture, particularly as it has been debated since the Lausanne Congress in 1974.

We do not ask you to choose between these two alternatives. The first one—pride in all that's American—happens frequently enough to be worrying, but I trust it is not the majority sentiment in this convention. The second, which is a denial of American culture, is not healthy for your dignity as persons and is probably impossible anyway.

There is a *third* way. What we are asking of you is to affirm what is positive in your being American and to be sensitive to what is negative. We trust that we are speaking the truth to you in love. Please listen to us because we are your brothers in Christ who greatly desire to be your partners in the worldwide mission of the church. Your mission is our mission, too.

What qualifications do messengers need if all nations are to obey and believe Jesus Christ? I suggest three essentials: First is zeal for God's glory. Second is love for needy people. And third is concern for the unity of the body.

Zeal for God's Glory

The first qualification for messengers is zeal for God's glory.

In Acts chapter 17, Dr. Luke tells us about the apostle Paul in Athens. Paul was waiting for Timothy to join him from Berea. While waiting in Athens, he looked around the city and was provoked as he saw that the place was full of idols. Provoked by idolatry! Dr. Luke uses a strong medical word: Paul had a paroxysm— his heart raced wildly within his breast as he saw the city's idols. He was full of righteous indignation from intense jealousy for the honor of the Lord Jesus. Promptly, he preached to the Athenians about Jesus and the resurrection.

Are you and I really convinced that God the Father has given to his Son Jesus the name Lord, the name which is higher than any other name, not only in this age but even in that which is to come (Eph. 1:21; Phil. 2:9-11)? Are we convinced that right now, the

54

same Lord Jesus is seated at the Father's right hand—the place of highest honor and supreme authority? Do we believe that the Lord Jesus whom we serve is indeed the King of the whole universe? If so, like Paul we should be cut to the heart—suffer a paroxysm—whenever we contemplate the vast numbers of people who do not bow the knee to the Lord Jesus today. Think about it: some three billion people out of the world's four billion do not acknowledge Jesus as their Lord. Many of them do so because they have never properly heard of who Jesus is and of what he has done for them.

Such a vast multitude would rather worship their ancestors or a piece of wood or stone or some godless ideology or even the material goods of this world, rather than the Lord Jesus! This must drive us to greater zeal in sharing the good news.

"Woe is me if I do not preach the gospel" (1 Cor. 9:16)! For I deprive the Lord Jesus of the honor due his name. He alone is worthy of all "blessing and glory and wisdom and thanksgiving and honor and power and might" (Rev. 7:12). Evangelism is persuading men and women to recognize Jesus for who he is in order that they may bow before him and acknowledge him as Lord and Savior. Messengers of the evangel need more zeal for God's glory if all nations are to believe and obey the Lord Jesus.

But how often our zeal comes from mixed motives. Horatius Bonar (1808-1889), Scottish preacher and hymn writer, had a dream. He dreamt that the angels took his zeal and weighed it and told him it was excellent. It weighed up to 100 pounds, all that could be asked. He—in his dream—was very pleased at the result. But then the angels wished to analyze his zeal. They put it in a test tube and analyzed it in various ways, with this result:

14 parts were from selfishness
15 parts were due to sectarianism
22 parts from ambition
23 parts because of love for humanity, and
26 parts from love for God

Bonar woke up humbled at the thought, and dedicated himself anew.

Are we zealous for Christian service? We must be, for we are here. It must be missionary zeal that led us to this convention in the first place. But if our zeal were analyzed by the angels, what would be the results?

How much of our zeal comes simply from the American value system: the pioneering spirit that stakes out unclaimed territory, the rugged individualism that insists on doing one's own thing, the fierce competitiveness that delights in besting the competition? How much of our zeal would come from the party spirit? I am not only a flag-waving Filipino nationalist. I am also a Bible-believing Baptist and an Inter-Varsity partisan to boot! How much of our zeal comes from a desire to build a religious empire with headquarters in America and branches in a hundred nations? How much of our zeal comes from an emotional need to do something in order to feel useful?

What per cent of our zeal truly comes from a *burning* desire to promote the glory of God?

Genuine zeal for God's glory is costly, but it will cost us only our pride and our selfishness. God grant that we have less and less of both. Genuine zeal for God's glory can stand criticism—such as I have expressed—for criticism only serves to purify it, like fire purifies gold. Let the testing of our zeal produce purer motives, like gold, much fine gold.

My North American brothers and sisters in Christ, I ask you to send missionaries to the ends of the earth who are zealous for the glory of God alone.

Love for Needy People

The second essential qualification for messengers is love for needy people.

We live in a world of incredible human needs. Hundreds of millions of people are poor and hungry, homeless and illiterate, battered by illness and die young. From Vietnam, people are prepared to risk their lives to escape on rickety boats adrift at sea or live in overcrowded refugee camps with no facilities, to search for a better life. In our day we may be seeing the extinction of the people of Kampuchea, as both young and old die off because help that comes is too little and too late. There are many other examples elsewhere in the world of people in great need of the most basic necessities.

You come from the world's richest economy, the largest consumers of the world's goods and of its energy. Does the contrast mean anything to you?

James, the brother of the Lord, wrote these words to the early Christians:

This is pure and undefiled religion in the sight of our God and Father, to visit orphans and widows in their distress, and to keep oneself unstained by the world. . . . What use is it, my brethren, if a man says he has faith, but he has no works? Can that faith save him? If a brother or sister is without clothing and in need of daily food, and one of you says to them, "Go in peace, be warmed and be filled"; and yet you do not give them what is necessary for their body; what use is that? Even so faith, if it has no works, is dead, being by itself. (Jas. 1:27; 2:14-17)

Please do not send to us missionaries who insist on a dichotomy between evangelism and social concern. Missionaries who teach that evangelism is our main or even sole concern. Missionaries who say that ministry to the temporal needs of people will also be done, but only as we have time, and as our limited resources allow.

Such missionaries make it difficult for us to defend the gospel against the Marxist charge that Christians promise a pie in the sky for the by and by. That Christians who have links with the West are but tools of Western imperialism, perhaps innocent, but helping to perpetuate the pockets of privilege, leaving the wretched of the earth to remain wretched!

We must not simply react to Marxist criticism, even though I realize that for many of you Marxism is a theoretical question, while for us the Communist system is a live and attractive option. If it can feed the hungry millions, why not, why not? But we are not simply reacting to Marxist criticism. Rather, we must come to realize that unless our love is demonstrated in practical terms of helping to meet the need for daily bread, our gospel of love will eventually sound hollow and unconvincing.

Am I pleading for a return to the old social gospel? No, no. I myself trained as a medical doctor but abandoned the profession in order to become a preacher of the gospel. But I do ask you to resist

—to fight—every dichotomy between preaching the gospel of love and demonstrating that love for needy men and women through good works. It was General Booth, founder of the Salvation Army, commenting on James 1, who said: "We will wash it [our money] in the tears of the widows and orphans and lay it on the altar of humanity."

I have long admired the Salvation Army and their twin emphases on soup and salvation. They have much to teach us all. They follow the example of the Lord Jesus closely. For he who came to give his life for our redemption also fed the hungry, healed the sick and welcomed the outcasts of society. He is still our model. His mission is our mission.

I know that those who urge us to do evangelism only are fired by the urgency of the evangelistic task. I share their sense of urgency. In the words of the 1974 Lausanne Covenant: "More than 2,700 million people, which is more than two-thirds of mankind, have yet to be evangelized. . . . Missionaries should flow ever more freely from and to all six continents in a spirit of humble service. The goal should be, by all available means and at the earliest possible time, that every person will have the opportunity to hear, understand, and receive the good news."

Nevertheless, this section of the Covenant, entitled "The Urgency of the Evangelistic Task," goes on to say: "We cannot hope to attain this goal [of world evangelization] without sacrifice. All of us are shocked by the poverty of millions and disturbed by the injustices which cause it. Those of us who live in affluent circumstances accept our duty to develop a simple life-style in order to contribute more generously to both relief and evangelism."

Both relief and evangelism. We cannot, we *must* not divorce the urgency of the evangelistic task from our duty to help those in need of daily bread.

What does this mean for us today, to us gathered here to consider missionary service? It means facing the question: How can I, as a follower of the Lord Jesus, live more simply today in order to give more to help meet both the temporal and eternal needs of so many people on this planet? Some of you have had the opportunity to skip lunch in order to help feed the hungry. Praise the

Lord for such opportunities! However, let our act be more than a token undertaken only in missionary conventions, perhaps under considerable social pressure. Let our act be a sign of a commitment to a simpler lifestyle so that we can be more generous in sharing our goods.

Let me assure you, my brothers and sisters, that the question is no less demanding on me as it is on you. For I know large numbers of people who live on much less of this world's goods than I do.

Concern for the Unity of the Body

The third essential qualification for messengers is concern for the unity of the body.

In his great treatise on the church, Paul appealed to Christians to be "diligent to preserve the unity of the Spirit in the bond of peace" (Eph. 4:3)—not just to be willing to maintain the Spirit-given unity of believers, but to be eager to do so. It is a lovely picture word, *diligent* or *eager* (RSV). It means to spare no effort. The picture it brings to my mind is that of a miler setting the pace, at the head of the pack, doing the last lap. Coming to the last two hundred meters, he will pull out all the stops. It is time to give it all he has got! He will spare no effort.

Sadly, the missionary enterprise has not been noted for great effort in either maintaining or nurturing the unity of the body. R. Pierce Beaver, the well-known missions historian, was quoted in a paper given at the Lausanne Congress on World Evangelization as saying, "More and more I am convinced that exported divisiveness is the greatest hindrance to the spread of the gospel in the non-Christian world."

The church is a reality in nearly every place in the world where we want to send missionaries. We need to come to terms with her. We must be willing to recognize her as our partner. She may be financially poor, theologically unsophisticated and inefficient in her methods, but she is not our inferior. We cannot bypass her without sinning against the body. Paul reminds us that there is only *one* body (Eph. 4:4) with only one head, the Lord Jesus.

Ah, but someone says, some parts of the body are closer to the head. This person says that we have been given a grand vision for fulfilling the Great Commission, and we have the resources of the mightiest nation on earth for carrying it out. It is only sensible to conclude that the most efficient way to finish the job is to ask the rest of you to join us!

Perhaps we do not say these things. We only act this way. Our actions speak louder than our words: *West is best!* Is this simply bad theology or is it American pride?

One day, a Western missionary said to me in church: "Tomorrow we are sponsoring a youth march for Jesus in Plaza Miranda [downtown Manila]. Why don't you come and join us and bring your students along?"

"Well," I said, "I am not sure that that is the best way to demonstrate the reality of the gospel in this season of student demonstrations."

"Listen," she said to me, "can we ever work together? This division between us is diabolical."

I very nearly said to her, "Yankee, go home!" It was a struggle to keep back the words.

My North American brothers and sisters in Christ: Can we ever be partners? *Partners.* Why do you keep saying that you have a master plan for fulfilling the Great Commission and you want us to join you in carrying out your plans? Why can't you come to us and say: "I have come in obedience to the Great Commission. How can you and I fulfill it together?" Partnership means a fellowship of equals.

A true partnership, a fellowship of equals, is not impossible. Sitting down together, discussing a plan of action in mutual respect and confidence is not an idle dream. In June 1980, some 650 Christian leaders from all over the world met in Pattaya, Thailand, for the Consultation on World Evangelization (COWE). COWE, which is sponsored by the Lausanne Committee, is a good illustration of a fellowship of equals both in planning and execution. The COWE Director is David Howard from the United States. The Program Chairman is Saphir Athyal of India, and the Lausanne Committee Executive Secretary is Gottfried Osei-Mensah of Ghana.

COWE is by no means the only example. For those of you who are not very familiar with it, let me commend to you the International Fellowship of Evangelical Students (IFES). Fifty autonomous, indigenous national student movements have banded together to spread the gospel in the student world. Examine the IFES structure, its pattern of authority and decision making, its choice of leaders. We are not anti-American in IFES. Last July, we elected as Chairman of the Executive Committee to serve until 1983, Dr. John W. Alexander. The IFES is not perfect, but you will discover a fellowship of equals.

China, that great nation of one billion people—nearly a quarter of mankind—is slowly opening its doors. What will be our plan of action? Is everyone going to jump on the China bandwagon and insist once again on doing his own thing? Or shall we manifest concern for the unity of the body and ask ourselves: "What kind of action by outsiders will be best for the Church in China? How can we enter into partnership with the Church in China in order to advance the spread of the gospel?"

It is for the sake of the unevangelized millions that messengers need to be concerned for the unity of the body.

Have I been harsh? Have I caused you pain? I can only trust that our exercise tonight has been essential surgery. I pray that the Holy Spirit, the skilled surgeon, will apply the needed pain in a therapeutic way to help the body become healthier. So that the one body—you and I and the people of God across the world—may together proclaim to all nations that there is salvation in no one else, that there is no other name under heaven given among people by which we must be saved, except the name Jesus. Amen.

Isabelo Magalit is associate general secretary for the International Fellowship of Evangelical Students and general secretary of Inter-Varsity Christian Fellowship of the Philippines. This address was originally given at the Urbana 79 student missions convention and appeared in Believing and Obeying Jesus Christ, *©1980 by Inter-Varsity Christian Fellowship of the U.S.A.*

6

That Amazing Thing Called the Church

Gordon MacDonald

If you really want to get serious about the matter of God's mission in the world, sooner or later you have to deal with the great fact of the church. If your heart is set on confronting people with the claims of Jesus Christ, leading to the possibility that they will choose to follow him, sooner or later you will have to deal with the great fact of the church. And if you are one of those who finds excitement in giving spiritual leadership to one or more believers so that they will grow in Christian maturity, sooner or later, you are going to have to deal with the great fact of the church.

This repetitive insight may leave a few people discomforted since it has been common recently for some Christians to pursue what might be called a churchless Christianity. And why not? Church has indeed been a joyless experience for more than one student. It is not unusual to hear the traditional liturgy of the anti-church man or woman who begins with the reasoning, "I was forced to go when a child," move on to "there was too much bickering and hypocrisy when I was a teen-ager" and conclude with a crescendo, "frankly, the church seems out of step with the world in which I live."

If I am familiar with these phrases, it is not so much that I have repeatedly heard them as much as the fact that I once employed them to describe my own attitudes toward the church and to justify why I found Sunday morning a choice occasion for catching up on what I thought was much-needed sleep. Besides, local Bible studies, leadership training groups and a host of friendships with other Christian students seemed to meet whatever need I had in the pursuit of corporate faith. So, I reasoned, the church was quite expendable.

Frankly, to think like that was bad theology and poor judgment on my part. I had some learning to do. I have to admit that the learning did not come easily either. The church in its congregational form does not always make it simple for one to come to positive conclusions about its importance in the scheme of eternal things. Here and there its history is sullied with some poor examples of the way things happen among the people called by God's name. And if one centers his or her attention on one or two local experiences in the past, or on a few generalizations often made about the irrelevancy of the church, it becomes easy to avoid confronting the issue of the church.

A serious study of the Scriptures on the question of God's program in the world became a shaking experience for me. What I discovered was a surprising continuity of principles which all pointed to the importance of my being heavily involved in the planting and maintenance of the church in its congregational form wherever God chose to place me. Among the principles which modified my earlier naive antithetical attitudes toward the church were these.

First, God has always had a "people." There has always been someone in the world with whom God chose to be in fellowship and through whom he would convey a redeeming message of love to those who would be willing to hear. In the earliest days of biblical history, the "people" were individuals such as Adam, Eve, Abel, Enoch, Noah and others. They shared a special insight into God's person and plan. It was not that they were better than anyone else, but they were presented with a responsibility which they generally accepted.

There followed a period of biblical history in which God spoke to *and* through a family—the extended family of Abraham. The twelveth chapter of Genesis enlarges this when God calls Abraham to leave his roots and embark upon a journey whose destination is unknown to him. Imbedded in the call is a challenge for Abraham to be a "blessing" to the world and the assurance that if he is obedient, his progeny will remain a "blessing" in the world.

That is exactly what happened. Abraham entered into a faith relationship with God, obeyed him, and was blessed in his old age with a son, Isaac. For a period of three generations God looked over the fortunes of this small group of people, protecting them, whispering into them new awarenesses of the meaning of worship and service.

Now some of those in Abraham's family—most notably Jacob—were not the finest specimens of holiness. There was duplicity, competition and outright crudity in some of their family relationships. But God persisted in his love for them, and they remained his people.

From the seed of Jacob came twelve sons who ultimately became the forebearers of the nation of Israel, a rather motley group of oppressed people who ended up living in Egypt for four hundred years. During those years, knowledge of the God of Abraham dwindled to almost nothing. What held them together primarily, beyond their racial affinity, was the oppression they were forced to endure at the hand of a succession of cruel Egyptian pharoahs.

But then there was that miraculous exodus, led by Moses, which drew them out from under oppression and to the foot of Mt. Sinai where they were once again reacquainted with their God. Among the very first things they were taught was something about their "peopleness." "If you will obey my voice and keep my covenant, you shall be my own possession among all peoples;

for all the earth is mine, and you shall be to me a kingdom of priests and a holy nation" (Ex. 19:5-6).

It must have been an awesome moment when this promise and challenge first sank into their spirits. These ragged and despised people were being called out by God to be priests and holy people. Later God would say to them, "you are the people of God," and that stamp upon them would mark their entire lives.

The story of the Old Testament is really nothing more than a description of the fortunes of the people of God, how they performed with brilliance on occasions and how they failed spectacularly on others. When they became ineffective in the later years through their resistance to God, he allowed them to face the consequences of their poor choices. The close of the Old Testament finds God's people struggling to come to grips with their specialness and their misuse of privileges given them.

I am convinced that Jesus Christ came partly to bring back to awareness the role and mission of the people of God. You could say he was the perfect "people." His sense of mission and his way of life plainly identified what he expected from men and women who wished to be God's people. An enormous amount of his time was taken up with the training of twelve men who, upon his ascension, became the founders of an enlarged dimension of the people of God, the church in Jerusalem, which quickly spread to other parts of the world.

Consider the plan the disciples-become-apostles implemented. Jesus gave them many commands on this before he left them to the power of the Holy Spirit. It is exciting to trace the growing awareness of these apostles, to see them discover that their mission was to preach the gospel *and* plant congregations. Evangelism was more than just leading people to Christ; it was bringing people into discipleship—and that meant relationship with one another as much as personal spiritual growth. Out of that emerged a further sense of mission as newly planted congregations moved out to plant still more congregations.

Later Peter would write of this incredible movement which melted Jews and Gentiles, rich and poor, slave and free, "You are a chosen race, a royal priesthood, a holy nation, God's own

65

people, that you may declare the wonderful deeds of him who called you out of darkness into his marvelous light. Once you were no people but now you are God's people; once you had not received mercy but now you have received mercy" (1 Pet. 2:9-10).

Peter's statement is simply amazing. He has equated the church with the call given at Mt. Sinai centuries before. Obviously he sees the church right in line with the succession of relationships God has established through the years with individuals, families, a nation and now the church—the fullest, broadest form of redeemed humanity blessed with a mission, a relationship and heavenly privileges.

All of that makes one thing very clear to me. Being part of the church is being part of the people of God, and I need to understand both the privileges and responsibilities. I am part of an incredibly long and consistent chain of graciously called people.

Second, the church is a precious thing to God. When St. Paul was making his last visit in the area of Ephesus, he called a meeting with the leaders of the great congregation there. His agenda centered on the future of the church and its ongoing fidelity to matters of faith. In the midst of his talk with those spiritual leaders, Paul said this, "Take heed to yourselves and to all the flock, in which the Holy Spirit has made you overseers, to care for the church of God *which he obtained with the blood of his own Son*" (Acts 20:28).

Often we emphasize that Christ died for each of us as individuals. But I am astounded to hear Paul affirm that Christ died for the church. And here is the old apostle charging these congregational leaders with the importance of their maintenance of the church because it belongs to God, purchased by the blood of his own Son.

The first time I saw this, I was immediately rebuked for the number of times I had criticized the church and rebuffed it without realizing that God loved it even if it was like Jacob had been at times. Here Paul was placing a value upon the church, and the value was measured according to the blood of Jesus Christ. Could I dare to look at the church and see it any differently?

I was no less impressed when I discovered in Ephesians 4 that the Christ who had given his blood for the church then proceeded

esus. Then a bright and gifted witness, named Apollos, comes and contributes to the work they have begun.

Acts 19 gives extensive coverage of how the church grew under Paul's ministry. Luke carefully records the raw material that the Spirit drew together into a congregation. From among the intellectual and philosophical Greeks, the Jewish refugees, pagan idol worshipers and early converts of John the Baptist, God built his dwelling place in this key city.

Finally, Luke takes us to a quiet, intense scene in Acts 20:17. It is three and a half months after Paul's sudden departure, and he has called the leaders of the church to meet him in a retreat, twenty miles to the south, at Miletus. Paul confides to them the deep feelings, the fears and the hopes that he had when he was among them and exhorts them to follow his example. Their farewell is one of the most tender and intimate accounts recorded in Scripture.

It's a great opportunity for Inter-Varsity Christian Fellowship to spend the year of Urbana 84 exploring the life of this congregation from its tumultuous beginnings through its many struggles to the final commendations and severe warning in Revelation. We have the privilege of bringing our expectations into line with God's concerning what it is like to be a member of his church in this world.

At Urbana 84 the book of Ephesians will be a major focus. In the plenary sessions there will be four expositions emphasizing the first three chapters. Four small group Bible studies will focus on Ephesians 4, 5 and 6, emphasizing the practical aspects of Christian life and discipleship.

The epistles to Timothy, as mentioned earlier, round out some of Paul's teaching and encouragement to this young leader of the church at Ephesus. And at Urbana Onward conferences following the convention, Revelation 2 will be examined in small groups.

You may wish to study, personally or in a small group, *all* of the Scriptures relating to the church at Ephesus in preparation for Urbana 84. To help you get started Yvonne Vinkemulder has provided the following four studies which examine Acts 18, 19 and 20.

Pete Hammond is director of Evangelism for Inter-Varsity Christian Fellowship of the U.S.A.

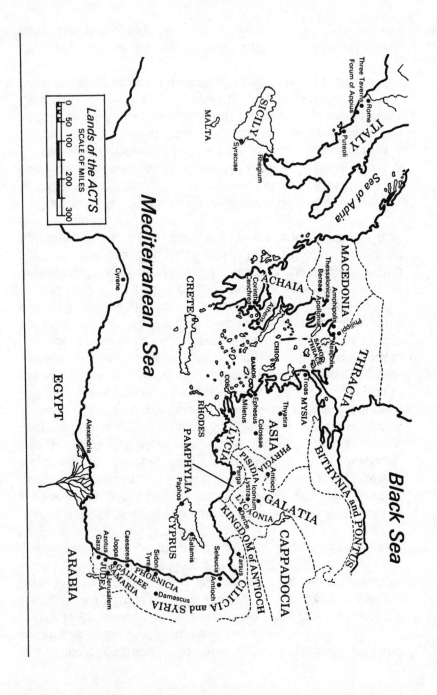

9

The Gospel Comes To Ephesus

Acts 18:18—19:7

Yvonne Vinkemulder

Read Luke 3:3-17. John the Baptist was the forerunner of Jesus Christ. His message to a tradition-bound people was radical: You cannot rely on your status as children of Abraham. Repent and bear fruit (that is, do works of repentance). His message prophesied the coming of Christ who would himself purify believers with the Holy Spirit.

In Acts 18:18—19:7 we see the re-education of an earnest evangelist, Apollos, and some eager disciples. Had they learned all that we know John taught? As you study this passage, reflect on *your* understanding of the gospel of Jesus Christ. Is it adequate? Have you clearly understood the essentials so you can teach others, as Aquila and Priscilla did? Or are you eager but lacking in understanding of the truth?

1. Skim through Acts 18:18—19:7 noting all the facts you can find about Paul, Priscilla and Aquila and Apollos.

What did each contribute to the evangelism of Ephesus? How do they complement each other?

2. Luke 3:3-17 tells us that John was preparing the way for Jesus. This preparation included preaching a "baptism of repentance for the forgiveness of sins" (v. 3) and urging the people to demonstrate their repentance by markedly changed behavior (vv. 8-14). After Jesus had come, why do you think the teaching of "John's baptism" was inadequate (Acts 18:24-26)? (If you have extra time, compare Luke 3 with Peter's sermon in Acts 2:14-39, noting the new concepts which were known after Jesus' death and resurrection.)

3. What effect did Priscilla and Aquila's instruction have on Apollos' future ministry? (Notice in verse 27 how he helped "those who by *grace* had believed.") How would you have responded to an interruption of your work?

4. Paul returned to Ephesus after Apollos left and found some "disciples" (Acts 19:1-2). Where do you suppose these disciples got their knowledge and beliefs?

5. John baptized with water but prophesied that Jesus would come and baptize with the Holy Spirit and with fire (Lk 3:15-17). What does this tell you about the difference between John's baptism and being baptized in the name of the Lord Jesus?

6. In this passage we've seen how Priscilla, Aquila and Paul detected and corrected error. We've also seen that Apollos was fervent, zealous, accurate in his teaching as far as it went, and able to significantly influence others. Why is it important that a missionary have a thorough understanding of the entire content of the gospel? What are the essentials of the gospel which a person should know and believe in order to become a disciple?

7. What can you do to improve your understanding of the gospel during the next week?

10

The Church Formed Despite Difficulty

Acts 19:8-20

Yvonne Vinkemulder

Ephesus, a mixture of Greek and oriental cultures, was the major center of commerce and religion in the province called Asia (note map of what is now Turkey). Strategically located on the seacoast, it was connected by highway with chief inland cities. It appears to be only one of two cities in this large province mentioned in Paul's missionary journeys. That the gospel was effectively planted can be recognized from the fact that the seven churches described in Revelation 2—3 are all located in this province. As you read Acts 19:8-20, try to discover the factors that caused the word of God to grow from its inauspicious beginning with a dozen disciples to multiple churches throughout the region.

1. Paul began his work in Ephesus in the synagogue (vv. 8-10). If you were Paul, how would you have felt in this situation? Why was the move to the "lecture hall of Tyrannus" strategic? How did the different audiences respond?

2. What other form of opposition did the gospel encounter according to verses 13-16? Why do you think these Jewish exorcists began to work in the name of the Lord Jesus? Why did they fail?

3. Why is imitation a threat? How does its exposure in this instance affect the growth of the gospel (vv. 17-20)?

4. What in our world today would be comparable to the practices these new believers abandoned?

What practices should you confess and rid yourself of? What can you expect God to do in response?

5. In this passage there are at least three forms of opposition to the gospel: disbelief (vv. 8-10), imitation (vv. 11-16) and occult practices (vv. 13-19). Identify factors that caused the gospel to triumph over each.

6. Can you think of times when you've sensed opposition to the gospel but saw the Word of God grow and prevail in spite of it? What effect did this have on you?

7. How does this passage enlarge your understanding of the missionary's task and your desire to help in it? Take time to pray for some missionaries by name, as well as for yourself and any difficult circumstances you may be facing.

11

The Gospel under Organized Attack

Acts 19:21—20:1

Yvonne Vinkemulder

Artemis (Diana to the Greeks) was the chief goddess of Asia and was considered to be the omnipresent "mother of all life." The temple in Ephesus was her chief shrine and controlled the business interests of the city. It had vast landholdings and operated the fisheries. Its priests and priestesses were wealthy bankers. It employed hosts of people, including craftsmen like Demetrius, who made and sold images and shrines of the goddess to assure pilgrims to the temple of her constant presence. Their real purpose was not religious but economic. They desired the benefits the trade brought to the temple and Ephesus.

As you study this passage, imagine you are in a large modern metropolis, comparable in influence to Ephesus in Paul's time. Imagine these events as if you were there watching them.

1. Read Acts 19:21—20:1. Describe the scene in downtown Ephesus.

2. In rallying the tradesmen, what threats did Demetrius pinpoint (vv. 24-27)?

To what extent do you think each threat may have contributed to the ensuing riot?

3. Where might you find organized opposition to the truth concerning Jesus Christ today?

4. Consider the riot described in verses 28-34. What do you learn about the dynamics of the mob reaction?

Paul wanted to get into the middle of it, but his friends wanted him to stay out. Which was the wiser course? Explain.

5. What do you think might have happened to the Christians in Ephesus had the riot continued?

How did God intervene?

6. In 19:21 Paul intended to leave Ephesus soon to continue his mission. In 20:1 he actually left. The writer doesn't detail his "encouraging" words to the Ephesians here. Had you been Paul, what do you think you might have felt and said?

7. Can you think of any religious, economic or political factor that tends to affect evangelistic work today? Have you personally experienced one?

8. What have you learned from Acts 19 about recognizing and dealing with spiritual conflict?

9. Take time to pray for (a) yourself as you attempt to live out and teach the Word of God in a secular culture and (b) missionaries and Christians in younger churches around the world known to be facing organized resistance to the Word of God.

12

The Church's Leadership Strengthened

Acts 20:13-38

Yvonne Vinkemulder

Having spent more time in Ephesus than any other city, Paul moved on to consolidate the work in Greece. He hoped to return to Jerusalem in time for Pentecost with a generous offering from the mission churches for the beleaguered mother church. (Pentecost, an ancient Jewish festival, had become an important celebration to the Christians also, as seen in Acts 2.)

Read Acts 20:13-38 and try to imagine Paul's reasoning as he decided to bypass Ephesus.

1. Having invested three years of his life in Ephesus, Paul was torn between going back or bypassing it. How did he resolve his dilemma (vv. 16-17)?

2. What were some of the more significant aspects of Paul's ministry in Ephesus according to verses 18-21?

What do you learn about his missionary strategy? About his character as a messenger of the gospel?

3. Reflect on his opening words in verse 18. If you were to say to former associates, "You know how I lived while I was with you . . . ," what personal history would you add?

4. According to verses 22-24, how did Paul's supreme aim in life affect his attitude toward circumstances? How does your aim in life compare with Paul's?

How do you react when you face hardships?

5. What dangers did he predict for the future of the church (vv. 29-30)?

What strong advice did he give the church leaders which would enable them (and us) to avoid these dangers (vv. 28, 31-35)?

6. Why did Paul have confidence in these leaders (v. 32)?

7. What leadership responsibility has been given to you?

What is your source of strength when faced with obstacles?

8. Visualize the final moments Paul and the Ephesian elders had together (20:36—21:1). What do their actions show about their relationship to each other?

How do you think they might have prayed for each other?

9. Pray for grace to live as transparently, speak as fervently and declare the gospel as completely as Paul, the messenger of the gospel, did.

Yvonne Vinkemulder is the head of Inter-Varsity's Legal Department.

Part III

The Urbana Convention

This part helps you think about yourself and your preparation for Urbana—or any other mission experience.

Michael Evans-Layng *gives you pointers on how to prepare for Urbana.*

William J. Treguboff *gives tips on getting the most out of the total Urbana experience.*

Pete Hammond *offers some practical helps for believing God and heading off problems at Urbana.*

Ken Shingledecker and James Rutz *provide hints on how to talk to mission agencies at the convention.*

13

Before You Go:
Getting Ready for Urbana

Michael Evans-Layng

Overwhelmed.

Never in my life had I been with 14,000 people for a week of intense learning. Never had I been so dramatically faced with the needs of our broken world and God's strategy for meeting those needs. Never had I been exposed to so many people from so many diverse backgrounds who were zeroed in on one thing: trying to understand what Jesus their Lord wanted them to do so that they could go out and do it.

What was the Urbana 73 missions convention for me? I was a junior at the University of California at San Diego when I attended that, my first, Urbana. I'll not forget it: four days packed with experiences, sensations and information that changed my life in fundamental ways. To sum up what I gained, I might use the word *perspective* or perhaps *window*. I gained a new window on the world, a look at things—including myself—from God's perspective.

Hearing so much about the world's needs and about the lordship of Christ added up, strange as it may seem, not to a feeling of despair but to one of hope! I saw clearly for the first time that as acute as the world's needs are, our Lord is ready, willing and able to deal with them because he *is* Lord. I saw that his lordship does not make him some big Cosmic Scrooge, as Paul Little said, out to ruin everyone's fun. He is our hope and he has a spot somewhere for *me* in the grand scheme of things. Amazing!

Yet my feelings of being overwhelmed were not all positive. It was terribly easy to lose sight of that budding perspective he was building in the midst of all the seminars, the snow, the talks and the *people!* Getting ready for these things before coming to Urbana can help maximize the positive while you're there and allow the Urbana experience to have more impact in the long run. Preparing adequately is also an exercise in good stewardship of time, energy and money. Believe me. I've been there. Without some discipline it is all too easy for your resources to be needlessly squandered at a conference of the size and scope of an Urbana.

How can you prepare? If God wants you to go to Urbana, prayer is the place to start finding that out. If he does want you to attend, you can also count on the fact that he wants to use the convention to communicate some important things to you about himself, the world and you. Prayer *before* you plunge into all the hubbub will help you hear his voice *during* the hubbub. No less important, it will help you to be receptive to what he is driving at.

Having a prayer partner for all of this wouldn't be a bad idea either. Find someone to pray with (maybe weekly) about why you are going. If you want to go just because so many others are or to get a spiritual shot in the arm, your motives need some work. Pray that you'll go because God wants you there. Pray about the financial need. Pray about your openness to learn once you're there. And don't forget to pray for the convention itself.

Second, read. Read carefully through this book. Get into a small group that will go through these articles and the Bible studies. If you can't find one, you might think about starting one. And if you're a bookish sort of person, you might want to tackle *Christian Mission in the Modern World* by John Stott (IVP). If you're really brave, try a missionary biography. You might be surprised at what you find.

Third, I would encourage you to find a missionary and ask him or her some questions. For instance, "How did you know that God was calling you to the mission field? How did you prepare? What is your personal vision for the work you're involved in? How do you spend your time on the field? Off the field?" Also ask his or her opinion on some of the current issues in the world of missions. "How do you respond, and why, to the call from some church leaders in the Third World for a moratorium on sending missionaries from the West? What do you think about self-supporting missionaries vs. missionaries sent from a mission board and financially supported by people from their home country? How do you feel about the Church Growth people and their call for evangelizing within homogeneous cultural groups?"

Fourth, consider using multimedia tools from TWENTYONE-HUNDRED Productions for your church or campus group. A variety of shows are available to widen your view of the world and the challenge to reach it. A creative and entertaining way to inform and motivate. Rental information is available from TWENTYONE-HUNDRED Productions, 233 Langdon, Madison, WI 53703.

Fifth, be sure to bring a checkbook or some extra cash for the offering that will be taken for student work overseas and to purchase books that will be available in the Armory.

Finally, come as rested as possible. Don't plan other draining events into your calendar for the two weeks preceding the convention. Get lots of sleep. You may have finals and Christmas activities to contend with, but realize that Urbana is very intense physically and emotionally. You need to be in shape to run the good race.

Have a good time preparing for Urbana! It is my prayerful desire that you will be sensitive to God's will not only concerning Urbana but also concerning the larger matter of your life as a whole.

Michael Evans-Layng served as a staff member with Inter-Varsity Christian Fellowship in California. This article originally appeared in You Can Tell the World, *© 1979 by Inter-Varsity Christian Fellowship of the U.S.A.*

14

Once You're There: Making the Most of Urbana

William J. Treguboff

Urbana is a total experience—physically, emotionally, intellectually, spiritually. It is exhilarating and draining in each of these ways. There are a few practical things you can do to make sure the "drain" doesn't overwhelm the "exhil."

Take emotions, for example. You know—love, hate, fear—and all those people. Well, one of the drain-type emotions possible at Urbana is feeling lost. With 17,000 of "them" and one of you, it's understandable. Of course, the way to combat lostness is with companionship which can help produce security. (That's an exhil-type emotion, by the way.) And right in the convention schedule are ways to get companionship. Each morning you will meet for a small group Bible study with about nine other people from your living unit. Each evening you will meet again with the same people for a time of sharing and prayer. This small group will become a crucial part of your Urbana experience as it gives you an opportunity to talk about what you are hearing, thinking and feeling with a few people who are experiencing the same things. The members of your small group can become your best friends at Urbana.

Then there's a little trickier drain-type experience you're likely to meet up with. It's the I've-been-standing-in-line-a-long-time-and-my-feet-hurt-and-this-is-frustrating emotional/physical combination drain. You could be experiencing this the first day at registration or anytime during the week while waiting for a meal or while trying to get into a special workshop. Yet here's a chance to get to know a couple of new people, to exchange ideas, or perhaps to help someone who has other problems besides sore feet.

Not to bypass the gray-matter side of things, the topic of the convention is missions, and your brain will be challenged from many different angles. Read the program schedule carefully sometime during your first twenty-four hours. Set some priorities of things not to be missed. Get a grasp of the structure of events. If confusion or questions arise, seek out an Inter-Varsity staff member or your small group leader. Take time to pray too, to give your mind a rest before God. Allow him to bring a calm so you can focus your mind and heart once again.

You can make Urbana a visual experience in ways besides viewing the multimedia shows. Locate by sight some of the prominent landmarks of this large University of Illinois campus—the Assembly Hall, Huff Gym, the Armory. Then find them on the campus map in your convention program which you receive at registration. Locate your living unit and your designated dining area as you move about the campus with reference to the other recognized landmarks. (Doing this can also help prevent the feelings of lostness I spoke of earlier.)

The weather at an Urbana convention can be quite cold—sometimes temperatures can fall below zero, accompanied by a side order of snow and wind. For people unaccustomed to cold or severe weather this can be somewhat of a shock. If you are not familiar with and accustomed to a midwestern winter, talk to people who know what ice and snow are like. Ski enthusiasts might offer suggestions for what is advisable and practical for potential Urbana weather. Aim for clothing that will provide you with warmth (layers of clothes, not one big coat), mobility and comfort, rather than exotic paraphernalia.

When all is said and done, Urbana is mostly a matter of attitude: a willingness to risk yourself in a new and unique setting, an act of commitment to God beforehand, an attitude of initiative in becoming familiar with a program and a schedule, and a spirit of inquiry about surroundings, people and events. Are you surprised that these attitudes are the same ones needed by a missionary experiencing the uniqueness of a culture for the first time? Your attitude and tactics in relating to surroundings, people, geography and weather can in itself be a parable of a missionary experience.

May God be with you as you stride across campus, as you sit in the Assembly Hall, as you stand in line, as you chat and pray with people, and as you hear his voice and experience his love during that week.

William J. Treguboff, formerly on staff with Inter-Varsity Christian Fellowship, is currently working towards a Marriage and Family Counseling License in California. This article originally appeared in You Can Tell the World, ©1979 by Inter-Varsity Christian Fellowship of the U.S.A.

15

Hints for Handling an Abnormal Blessing

Pete Hammond

I have attended six Urbana gatherings and numerous other conferences for believers. They can be a blessing or a blight. It is not a normal experience to gather with so many of God's children this side of heaven. As good stewards we need to take special measures to honor the privileges. Here are some hints.

Believe God:

☐ to guide you by careful study of the schedule before you get to Urbana and then daily during the convention. Note that the focus of each day's major meetings is as follows: Day 1—Faithful to the Task; Day 2—Faithful to the People of the World; Day 3—Faithful in Our Commitment; Day 4—Faithful as a Christian.

☐ to fill your life with new friends at meals, in your Bible study group, and while traveling together. Decide now to get to know them and to share yourself with them.

☐ to change and broaden your thinking about yourself, your career and your values. Think hard about your future. Write down your reactions each day and share them with your prayer group. Think them through when you get home, too.

☐ to equip you to help students from your school who could not attend, relatives back home, your home church when you return. In other words, look at yourself as attending for the sake of others. Get materials they can use too. Pray daily for them.

☐ to use your INTERCRISTO print-out to help sort out lots of good information about ministry, mission agencies and opportunities. (See more in the next article.) Go to the Armory the first day just for orientation, then seek out key connections the following days.

Oppose the World, the Flesh and the Devil:

☐ by eating decently—that is at least two good, slow meals a day while at Urbana and during travel. Drink lots of fluids. The heated buildings tend to dehydrate you.

☐ by sleeping each night. Sleep is spiritual.

☐ by spending a time alone with God each day praying, meditating in Scripture (using the material that will be provided) and thinking through the day.

☐ by sharing your needs, reactions and questions freely with a prayer partner and your Bible study/prayer group.

☐ by asking hard questions gently of yourself, friends, speakers and, especially, the missionaries.

☐ by being sensitive to others and seeking to understand those who are insensitive or offensive. Seek help from your small group leader or one of the staff if you need it.

☐ by pacing yourself through all the meetings, taking notes of key ideas and then buying the compendium for review and sharing with others.

This is probably the largest temporary family you'll ever be a part of. Rejoice in the riches, respond gently to the differences, and praise God together.

Pete Hammond is director of evangelism for Inter-Varsity Christian Fellowship of the U.S.A. This article originally appeared in Let Every Tongue Confess, © 1981 by Inter-Varsity Christian Fellowship of the U.S.A.

16

Talking with Mission Agencies

Ken Shingledecker and James Rutz

Each afternoon at Urbana you will have the opportunity to interact with representatives from more than 130 mission agencies. These representatives will be at mission displays in a massive building known as the Armory. Now, if you know what agencies you want to talk with and what questions you want to ask, your visit to the Armory can be very helpful. But if like most students, you do not have any idea what to ask or which to visit, you could find the crowded Armory just one exhausting experience. How can you avoid that?

First, when you register at Urbana you will be given a computer print-out produced in INTERCRISTO. This print-out will list about ten mission agencies whose displays you should visit. These agencies are determined by matching your abilities and interests (as indicated on your Urbana registration form) with the opportunities that mission agencies have available. You should use this print-out as your personal guide to the Armory.

Second, do not be intimidated by the large crowds around each display. If you cannot talk to an agency, visit some of the surrounding displays and then try again. Or you may want to attend some of the elective seminars or go take a nap and return to the Armory when it is less crowded. Crowds are usually thinner right when the Armory opens each afternoon and on the second and third full days of the convention.

Third, do not feel compelled to attack the Armory every afternoon of the convention. Plan your time so that you can avoid it altogether on one or more days. Try to meet with friends in some building other than the Armory so you do not have to fight the crowd. This will also make the crowd smaller for those who must go to the Armory.

Fourth, here are some tips on what information to seek from each agency.

Statement of Faith Although most nondenominational boards are conservative, they are not highly detailed in their doctrinal statements. Because of this, you will probably have little trouble agreeing with them on the basics if your theology is conservative. Further, you may be surprised to find that some denominations with a liberal membership have a missionary force that is quite conservative.

Countries Most missionary candidates have at least some feelings of preference for a certain field or area or type of subculture. But try not to be overly rigid because many boards will want to make strong suggestions about your location. Long experience shows that God often speaks to a candidate through a board!

Track Record How well is the agency doing? What has been its impact on the field? Has the work grown, especially in the last two years? Even though work is very slow in some countries, a board should have *something* to point to.

Size On the positive side, a small board has the advantages of a friendly, informal family. A large board has the fringe benefits of a solid, sophisticated organization. On the negative side, the sloppy methods of some small boards have helped to keep them small for decades. And the bureaucratic efficiency of some large boards could give you that lost feeling of being merely a cog in a big machine.

Importance   How needed is the board? What would happen to the progress of world evangelization if it disappeared? Just how much is riding on its success? Remember that some of the less dramatic types of work (for example, teaching missionaries' children) are in the background but nonetheless essential.

Goals and Management   Is the board moving in a clear direction? Do the directors actually help their people? It's difficult to tell just from publicity material; a dedicated field staff with all eyes on the Lord may stumble and flounder from one huge success to another for years, even though supervisory support is erratic.

Type of Work   Does the board actually need you? If you feel you should get into one particular type of work, make sure they want people in that line now! If you're more flexible, no problem.

Leadership   Who are the leaders, the guiding lights? How long have they been with the board? What is their reputation in the church? Don't be bashful about asking people from other boards about their leadership. You aren't digging up dirt; you're doing your homework wisely.

Organization   Is the board appointed? Elected? Is the whole show run by one man? Is it run as an oligarchy by one family? (Some fine small boards are.) And are they authoritarian, democratic or somewhere in between? Is the individual missionary's voice heard in policy discussions? What is their attitude toward women?

Origin   How and when did they get their start? As a natural outgrowth of the ministry of one person or small group? As a splinter from another board? As a new outreach by an established organization?

Standards   What qualities and qualifications must you have as a candidate? Does the board provide (or require) special training? The rule of thumb here is to seek out a board whose standards you just barely meet. Then you will be in the most outstanding organization that you could qualify for.

Turnover   How many years does the average missionary stay on? And where do they go after they leave—into some other no-

103

table work or into thin air?

Personnel Sources   Where do the candidates come from? One denomination? Several countries? The white-collar culture? If you were reared in the Oakland ghetto you may be broadened by working alongside exfarmhands from Missouri, but be prepared for a few adjustments.

Finances   What if you're in the Upper Amazon Valley and your support drops off one month? Is this board's financial policy sound? Is it open to the public? Are their contributors solidly behind them with a high per-person support figure? Is their overhead expense less than a quarter of the total budget?

Style   Finally, there is that indefinable business of *feel*. Are these your kind of people? If not, do you like them anyway? Are you comfortable with them? Talk with missionaries on furlough. Write to someone on the field in the country which interests you. Visit the field if you can. It's worth the effort; it's like picking out a new family.

Don't ever let yourself get bogged down, though, in the details of choosing a board. Remember, if God has called you to the field, then someone is waiting for you and will be hurting if you don't get there.

Ken Shingledecker is a missions specialist for IVCF-USA. He wrote the first half of this article, which originally appeared in Let Every Tongue Confess, *© 1981 by Inter-Varsity Christian Fellowship of the U.S.A.*

James Rutz is director of communications of Chuck Colson's Prison Fellowship ministry in Washington, D.C. He wrote the last half of this article, which originally appeared in the March 1980 issue of HIS magazine under the title "Check List for Missions," © 1980 by Inter-Varsity Christian Fellowship of the U.S.A.

Part IV

What's Next?

What can you do after learning so much about missions?

Robert Munger gives practical guidelines for getting to know the will of God for your life.

Warren W. Webster presents the advantages of working with mission agencies.

Ruth Siemens explores the new avenues of reaching the world's unreached.

Ned Hale gives you lots of how-to's for getting involved with international students.

Melvin J. Friesen happens to think everyone is called to help in Christ's global mission.

17

Knowing God's Will

Robert B. Munger

A fine young Christian man came to see me in my study one afternoon. "I'm faced with some important decisions. I've been reading my Bible and praying but don't seem to be getting any guidance from God. Time is running out on me. I don't know what to do!"

"Tell me about it," I replied.

"Well, I graduate in June in engineering. I have two good job offers—one in Utah, the other in California. I'm also considering giving two years as a short-term missionary overseas before making a long-term career commitment here in the United States. Most importantly, I've been going with a wonderful young Christian woman. She doesn't graduate for another year. I need to know if this relationship is of God before I graduate and leave."

There they were—three crucial, life-determining decisions cascading down on him at once. Vocation, location, marriage.

You may not be in such a crisis of decision, but most students are making major choices. How do we make right decisions? What process will assure us that we are doing God's will?

To gain a sense of God's direction for our lives, we must heed Jesus' words in his call to his disciples. First, we will note some of the basic principles of guidance found in his call. Then we will consider some practical procedures to help us get a good start toward fulfilling his intention for our lives.

Called to Follow a Person
In Mark 1:17 Jesus commanded, "Come, follow me!" (NIV). He did not say where he was going to lead his followers nor did he designate the place of their ministry. The call of Jesus is first and always to himself, to walk with him and be at his side. His first call is not to a particular mission or movement. He does not hand us a plan telling us exactly where we are to be or what we are to do at any particular moment. Rather, he offers himself, saying, "Follow me."

To gain a clear sense of direction and move out in today's world according to the will of God, we must begin with a wholehearted, irrevocable decision to follow Jesus Christ, to live for him, to be his. We offer ourselves up to him, to serve and please him supremely.

Called to a High Purpose
Nothing will give you more significance, meaning, dignity or value than the commitment to be Christ's—to be in his will and to do his work in the world. No matter how insignificant an individual may feel, to be linked to that purpose gives supreme significance. John tells us that "Whoever does the will of God abides for ever" (1 Jn 2:17 NIV). When you do the will of God, you are in a forever work that will last.

What are you going to do ten years from now? How much is it going to count a thousand years from now? If you have not thought through your intended vocation, you have some business to do with God. Are your plans in harmony with what God wants you to do so that you may fulfill his supreme purpose? You may not go to a foreign mission field. You may not be in a church vocation.

But be sure that you are led by God so that his purpose will be forwarded. Let us be fishers of men and women, in business for God.

It was during the summer following my graduation from the university that I started to follow Christ seriously. Since that time I often have reflected on that decision. Suppose I had chosen to live as many of my colleagues and pursue my own plans? Suppose I had settled for an easy life and personal happiness. What would my satisfactions be now, fifty years later? I am overwhelmed at the incredible grace of God that has given me a part in that work which abides forever. I am involved in the mission that fills an ordinary life with extraordinary meaning and brings immeasurable rewards in both time and eternity. To follow Christ is to be in the biggest and most rewarding business in all the world.

Called to a Powerful Partnership

"I will make you fishers of men," Jesus said to his disciples in Mark 1:17 (NIV). Could he mean it? Ordinary people? Sinful people? With hang-ups and failures and average abilities? "Yes," we can hear the Lord reply. "As I worked through you to catch fish, so I will work through you to catch people and do the greater work of God I came to fulfill. Simply follow me. Trust me and do what I say." They forsook all and followed him. As we now know, he did for them what he said he would do. He will do the same for you and me.

Jesus Christ is the Master Fisherman enabling those who follow him to do the work of God. He is also the Good Shepherd who guides and cares for those who trust themselves to him.

We need not be anxious about getting the right directions from God or be concerned about whether we will have the courage to follow his direction. Instead, we are simply to put ourselves in the shepherd's care. If we want to do his will, he will see to it that we have the necessary information and will put within us the desire and the energy to move out with him. He is even able to overrule past mistakes and in the process to mature us in Christian life and service. The words of the apostle Paul encourage us: "God is always at work in you to make you *willing* and *able* to obey his own purpose" (Phil 2:13 TEV).

109

If you are not certain that you have launched in response to the word of the Master Fisherman or question whether you have placed yourself in the care of the Good Shepherd, consider this suggestion. Prayerfully and carefully draft a statement of ownership recognizing the lordship of Jesus Christ over all you are and have, authorizing him to take whatever steps necessary to accomplish his will in and through you. Sign it. Settle it once and for all. Then continually remind him of his responsibility to keep that which has been entrusted to him (2 Tim 1:12).

Called to a Close Companionship

"He appointed twelve . . . that they might be with him," to be his companions (Mk 3:14 NIV). He wanted them to be alongside him in his saving mission, as personal friends. He was teaching and training them to one day carry his mission to the world. More than that, he loved them and desired their companionship just as he loves you and me and wants us to be close to him forever. He calls us not only for what he may bring to us and through us to the world but also for what we may bring to him.

In following Christ, my first struggle was to be willing to give up my personal plans, to leave family and friends and boats and nets, to follow him wherever he might lead. My second great struggle, which to me was more difficult than the first, was to give up my ambition to be a successful servant of Christ and humbly to be and do whatever he wanted. I was eager to achieve great things for God, to preach to crowds of people with numbers of converts and applauding saints. Lovingly he brought me to a deeper level of commitment by giving me a desire to be and do whatever pleased him. Here is the key to guidance: *we must be willing to do God's will before we know what it is*—to trust ourselves to him and to be taught, shaped and led as he shall choose.

Roll Up Your Sleeves

Now let us turn from principles to a few practical procedures. First *offer yourself daily to God*. "Present your bodies as a living sacrifice" (Rom 12:1). Each morning report to him, saying "Here I am. Do in me whatever needs to be done. I give you full authority to take whatever steps are necessary that I may be all that you want me to be and do all that you want me to do." He is completely reliable. He will take us at our word.

Second, *pray for guidance and grace.* Ask him to make his way plain to you and to put his desires within you (See Lk 11:9-13). In *Affirming the Will of God,* Paul Little suggests that you spend five minutes a day specifically asking God to show you his will (pp. 17-18).

Third, *inform the mind.* We are guided by the truth of God's Word. The Scriptures are a primary source of our knowledge of God. Here we learn about him and his will for our lives. Here Christ's Word addresses us and his grace promises to support us. We are guided also by the facts of God's world. People are guided by what they know, not by what they do not know.

We keep in touch with God's world through persons, periodicals, programs, missionary conferences and workshops. Do not neglect to read missionary biographies. Personal conversation with those in cross-cultural missions is also helpful. Best of all is a short-term or summer mission assignment, many of which are now available through various agencies and mission boards. Continually we are to lift up our eyes to see the fields of God's world, ripe, ready to harvest (Jn 4:35).

A fourth thing we should do to find God's will is to *join with other world Christians.* Jesus called his disciples to a committed company. We must not presume to be solitary followers of Jesus Christ. Seek the counsel of trusted believers. To move out step by step alongside our Lord with a bright faith and a warm heart, we need one another as fellow followers—praying for one another, supporting one another, seeking to love one another even as he has loved us (Jn 31:34-35).

Finally, you should *get going! Start now right where you are!* Sam Shoemaker had a hard-hitting formula for Christian living: "Get right with God! Get together! Get going!" We are called in Christ. We have been given his message. We are now in his service, entrusted with the everlasting gospel. Wherever our lives are touching people there is a God-given ministry with opportunity to listen, to love, to lift, to share and to serve. Flight across an ocean into another country or culture does not somehow change us. The statement is true, "Wherever you go, you are there!" When Jesus called his first followers he said, "Follow me" and started walking. If they were to follow him, they had to move. They left everything and followed. World opportunities are before us. Jesus is striding to enter them in love and power. He is calling us to follow.

Robert Munger, former professor of evangelism and church strategy at Fuller Theological Seminary, is associate pastor at Menlo Park Presbyterian Church in California.

18

The Messenger and Mission Societies

Warren W. Webster

In the process of world evangelization, one means that God has used to spread the gospel and plant churches in nearly every land is that of mission societies.

Mission societies are people who have banded together in a commitment to the Lord and to one another. They make special efforts to crosscultural frontiers in order to evangelize and disciple those who would not normally be reached with the gospel.

We know from Scripture that it is God's will that people and nations everywhere should be reached with the gospel. And so committed Christians across the centuries have felt free, under the Spirit's guidance, to use their God-given reason and creativity in organizing and using whatever structures are necessary to carry out God's purposes in fulfillment of the Great Commission.

Early in the New Testament, such as in Acts 13, we find embryonic mission structures functioning alongside local church assemblies. The organizational forms of both church and mission were simple. The New Testament primarily describes first-generation Christianity at a time when the mustard seed of faith had just begun to sprout and spread and had not reached full development. Paul's missionary bands have provided a prototype for subsequent mission organizations. Through these organizations the Lord's obedient disciples in succeeding generations have endeavored to carry out his Commission.

You and Mission Societies

In determining where and how you might go with the gospel to unreached peoples or to another culture, mission societies offer a number of advantages for your consideration:

1. Missions are church related. They arise out of churches and, in turn, produce more churches—often where previously there were none. This must be our top priority in missions because it was Christ's. It has been said: "The mission of the church is missions; the mission of missions is the church." In whatever role or capacity you go abroad, I urge you to be closely and vitally related to at least one church at home for prayerful backing and to some assembly of believers abroad for worship, witness and fellowship.

2. One great advantage of mission organizations is that they free witnesses for full-time ministry and long-term contacts with people. This provides time and opportunity for learning languages and cultures in order to communicate the gospel effectively. It is especially crucial for workers committed to Bible translation or called to witness in primitive and rural areas where self-support is extremely difficult.

3. Missions are able to utilize a broad range of spiritual gifts and abilities committed to the Master's use.

4. Mission agencies assume responsibility for planning, under God and in the light of his Word, as well as for supervising and evaluating progress toward goals set by prayer and faith.

5. Missions supply continuity to the work so it doesn't stop when one person leaves or has to withdraw. They also provide a sense of identity, community and fellowship for witnesses who might otherwise feel very much alone. Spiritual gifts exercised within the body complement one another.

6. Missions have been used of God as a reservoir for revival, keeping truths about the lostness of humankind, the finality of Christ and the urgency of evangelism uppermost in the life and outreach of the church.

7. Missions place a strong emphasis and dependence upon the power of prayer, the Spirit-filled life, personal evangelism and stewardship of life and resources.

8. Missions are responding with great flexibility and creativity to changing times. They introduced theological education by extension in the past decade and now are experimenting with gospel telecasts via satellites. They are leading the way in short-term programs for students and lay people. Some missions even have programs for liaison with self-supporting workers in secular jobs in order to provide fellowship.

9. Missions today are instilling in younger churches a vision for developing their own mission structures as sending churches.

One obvious disadvantage of traditional mission societies is that they are generally prohibited from functioning in so-called closed countries because of their visible profile. In such situations the efforts of visiting Christian students, tourists and self-supporting vocational witnesses are especially strategic.

In assessing the strengths and weaknesses of modern mission agencies, Dr. Ralph Winter of the U.S. Center for World Mission concludes that when it comes to crosscultural communication of the gospel "no one has invented a better mechanism for penetrating new social units than the traditional mission society, whether it be Western, African or Asian, whether it be denominational or interdenominational."

Just as not every Christian is called to be a missionary in a crosscultural sense, so mission societies are not for everyone who wants to serve the Lord abroad. The Lord uses many means and methods of sending out messengers with the good news. Since Americans in business overseas outnumber missionaries by one hundred to one, committed Christians should make every effort to infiltrate and utilize this vast reservoir of paid-for talent. The truth is that from this generation of Christian students in every land we need tens of thousands who will seriously commit themselves to world evangelization. And we need them both as full-time missionaries and self-supporting witnesses. Whether you go as an exchange student or lecturer, in commerce, industry or government, as an individual or part of a supportive team, as a full-time missionary or in a self-supporting role—the goal is the same: "that all nations might believe and obey Jesus Christ!"

Warren Webster is general director of the Conservative Baptist Foreign Mission Society. He served as a missionary in West Pakistan for 15 years.

19

The Messenger and New Avenues

Ruth Siemens

I am thankful to God for mission societies and the remarkable way he has used them in these last one hundred fifty years of amazing missionary advance. In view of the fact that mission agencies are effectively used by God, why should we bother to investigate secular options to overseas work at all?

These nontraditional avenues are needed because of the *nature of our task.* In spite of the wonderful fact that we are now a universal church, three-fourths of God's world is still enemy-occupied territory. Mission agencies are God's regular army, but we need guerrilla forces that can enter closed countries and infiltrate every structure of society. Only the layperson can do this. Because we are at war, one avenue is not enough, no matter how good. We must make creative use of *every* possible avenue God puts at our disposal.

Second, the *dimensions of our task* demand new avenues. Even where the church is established, each new generation must be won. Billions of people are currently beyond the gospel's reach.

Third, we need new, nontraditional avenues because of the cost of supporting a greatly increased missionary force. We can multiply the missionary force by ten, at no cost to the church, by making use of secular avenues.

Fourth, we need new avenues because of *closed countries.* Of the thirty-five thousand North American missionaries today, about 95 per cent work in only 17 per cent of the world. Only a couple of thousand work in 83 per cent of the world (Winter, *Seeing the Task Graphically,* Pasadena: William Carey Library). Some countries are tightly closed. Others greatly restrict missionary activity, and some are slowly closing. Yet there is not a single country that cannot be penetrated in some way through secular avenues.

Fifth, *our rapidly changing world* requires new avenues. Trends in decolonization, nationalism, resurgence of non-Western religions, urbanization, secularization, industrialization and education provide unprecedented opportunities. There are one hundred twenty new countries in the world less than thirty years old, seeking help for their development needs. Several million jobs are available to North Americans in these and in older countries as well. These are positions their own citizens cannot fill at this time. Some Western cults and non-Christian religious groups have been quick to use these opportunities. How tragic if Christians ignore these new avenues God puts at our disposal.

New Avenues Abroad

There are several new avenues to ministry abroad. The first is the *secular position abroad,* whether it is with a firm, a voluntary agency, a U.N., U.S. or national government agency or perhaps an educational or medical institution. Overseas Counseling Service now has computerized data on more than one hundred thousand secular positions. There are 526 job descriptions in 230 countries and territories, including the Middle East, Eastern Europe and the People's Republic of China.

The best positions require good degrees, marketable skills and experience. Some are for people in midcareer or retired people. Often there is no upper age limit. But there are many entry-level jobs as well. Careers most in demand are agriculture, engineering, medicine, business, teaching at every level—especially the sciences, math, industrial arts and English as a foreign language. A second new avenue is the *self-employed missionary,* who sets up his or her own business overseas. The first missionary ever who moved to a distant land to make God known was a wealthy cattleman named Abraham. Centuries later Priscilla and Aquila moved their tentmaking business from Rome to Corinth to Ephesus and back to Rome, and it maintained them and other missionaries.

There are *scholarships* for overseas undergraduate study and postgraduate study, even in closed countries. With the right combination of language and career, opportunities for advanced study and research are also available. Students are less suspect and have more liberty to speak out.

There are *internships, externships and other work-study programs* in most careers at little or no cost.

Summer service overseas should be seen mainly as exposure to another culture and training for missions, although God can use you even in two or three months. This can include work with any one of the mission boards that have such programs or with secular programs through your university.

A new avenue for older folk is *retirement abroad.* Their long experience can be put to good use. Older missionaries are needed in countries where age is held in great respect.

The Messenger in These New Avenues
Most of the objections to self-supporting and other nontraditional avenues of missionary work evaporate if we define our terms. Despite the fact that several hundred thousand evangelical Christians work abroad, most of them are not considered missionaries. When do American Christians employed or studying abroad qualify as missionaries?

First, genuine missionaries *make disciples.* This is the commission Jesus gave us. No matter what other ministries we have, we must also evangelize and disciple.

Second, genuine missionaries, professional or nonprofessional, have a *crosscultural ministry.* They identify with nationals, live among them, share their lives, learn their language.

Third, even with secular positions, such messengers understand they are *full-time missionaries*. They find opportunities off the job. But their main ministry is at work. They do their secular work not only for their human employers, but for Jesus Christ. They develop caring relationships with those around them. Their genuine concern and the integrity of their lives create thirst in their associates. Their message is credible because it has already been lived out before the eyes of their colleagues, under pressures, in concrete situations.

Fourth, even before going abroad, true missionaries witness to the people already around them on campus, at work, in the neighborhood. Faithfulness is God's prerequisite for further assignments.

Fifth, genuine missionaries *do not do their own thing*, but are well informed in advance on how God's troops are faring in the country to which they go, and they seek their counsel on how they can fit in.

Sixth, Christ's messengers *are sent*. They are convinced God has opened up this new avenue for them. His church and other Christian friends confirm that conviction by committing themselves to prayer on their behalf.

It is the messengers' *motivation* that counts and the *spiritual fruit* God gives them in their work. Recall Jesus' words after he had been seated on God's throne and given all authority in heaven and on earth. "Go, then, to all peoples everywhere [that is, wherever life under God's sovereignty takes you] and make them my disciples" (Mt 28:18 TEV). He also said, "Look at the fields" (Jn 4:35 NIV). We must gather information and find ways to go. God guides us largely through data we seek out and prayerfully evaluate.

Jesus Christ has opened new secular avenues for us to make sure that when we stand before his throne there will be representatives with us from all the peoples of the earth (Rev 7:9).

Ruth Siemens served as staff member-at-large with IVCF and worked for many years with IFES in Peru, Brazil, Portugal and Spain. She is the founder of Overseas Counseling Service.

20

Growing an International Friendship

Ned Hale

With the large and growing number of international students in North America (some estimate ten per cent of the entire student population by 1990!),we literally have every nation of the world represented on our campuses.

If your interest in missions has been stirred, one way to gain some practical learning experiences is to befriend a few of these international students on your campus. The rewards will be mutual! You will learn a great deal about how to relate to someone from another culture, and you will have the joy of discovering more about God's will for you as a missionary right here and now! The international will benefit immensely by discovering a Christian friend who not only can become like a brother or sister but who can become the channel by which God's love is seen and felt.

Personal Involvement

First things first. Where can you find international students? Attend the cosmopolitan club or other international student groups to learn about other cultures and to meet students. At the first of the year you can meet them as they arrive on the bus, train or plane. Offer your assistance to programs already going on campus which help international students to get oriented. Show them around campus. Help them find a residence and map out courses for registration. Explain some of the peculiar customs and traditions you run into.

When you start up friendships, be sure to learn full names correctly. Then find out on your own about their country, religion and customs. And don't be interested in them just to preach to them. If you do not intend to care about them as total persons, it might be best not to initiate the friendship at all. Since friendship expectations by most internationals are high, and you have only so much time to give, *a few close personal relationships* with internationals will accomplish more in the long run.

It's okay to feel inadequate too. If you don't know much about a person's country or background, simply ask them to tell you about it. You'll learn a lot, they'll enjoy telling you, and you'll convey real love by having a sympathetic ear!

Share the gospel while growing into friendship. Through trial and error it has been found that the best way to communicate religious truth to international students is by letting it be a natural part of a personal friendship over a period of time. There are several reasons for this. First, their primary emotional need in North American culture is for a close personal relationship with one whom they can implicitly trust. Second, because of the reputation of some American students' religious backgrounds (legalism, hypocrisy, and so on), internationals are apt to be distrustful of religious people until they can view the practical application of Christianity to daily life. Finally, one must presuppose a lack of knowledge in the foreign students about the Scriptures and biblical terms. You'll need many times together when you can talk about and clarify what the gospel means.

Once the friendship has begun, there are a variety of ways you can spend time with the person, helping your relationship to grow. For example, you could study together. Some international students welcome help with English. (You could also help with English through Bible study in a modern translation.) But realize that while many have learned formal English, they may have trouble understanding colloquial expressions. Or take an international student home with you over the holidays or during vacations. Especially plan to *bring* them to international holiday conferences held near Lake Tahoe, Bear Trap Ranch, Cedar Campus, Pioneer Camp, Banff and many other sites in North America (write IVCF for information). Finally, invite your friend to the regular social activities (banquets, picnics and so on) offered by your campus Christian fellowship.

Group Involvement
As a group, the place to begin is to commit yourselves to befriend international students. There are some practical ways you can fulfill this commitment.

Participate in the brother-sister program on your campus if there is one. If not, your fellowship could push to get one started through the student council or the college administration. This would involve writing to the students during the summer, meeting them when they come by train or bus, helping them to get acquainted with the campus and following through during the year.

Another possibility is to sponsor parties aimed at meeting internationals. Use these as opportunities to begin personal friendships. Consider having a tea for internationals twice a semester to gain initial contact with them on a social level.

If you advertise a speaker on a subject like "Christianity and Its Relevance to the Modern World," the interested foreign students will attend. Their degree of interest in spiritual things can be determined by their response to the speaker's offer of booklets after his or her talk. Students who want further information about Christianity can sign up for these. You then have a perfect opportunity for visiting the student personally, giving him or her the booklet free of charge and finding out in private conversation where the student is with God. Use this opportunity to build per-

123

sonal friendships and invite the students to other situations where Christian friendships can be cultivated and where they can become acquainted with Jesus Christ. Often this will encourage them to become involved in the ongoing fellowship of your group.

Once a semester, usually at the beginning, a student in your fellowship should get permission to use campus facilities for the tea and to advertise it. Invite a speaker and agree on a topic. Then arrange for refreshments to be served and for the advertising to be made and distributed to key places on campus. Then about one week before the tea, send a letter to each international student on campus inviting him or her to the tea. You might be able to get the addresses of the internationals from the foreign student adviser or the dean. Each Christian should be encouraged to bring at least one international to the tea.

You might also sponsor a dinner in which your campus fellowship buys the food and some internationals from one or two countries work together with your members to teach them how to prepare an international meal. Or try inviting internationals to the home of a faculty member for a home-cooked meal and to hear the faculty member speak on "What Basic Christianity Is." Most internationals want to learn about Christianity and its relationship to our culture. Encourage informal discussion so that questions may be answered.

Another idea is a progressive dinner in the homes of various Christians from local churches who are interested in befriending foreign students. This can be an excellent way of introducing the Christian community to this ministry. Each Christian student should bring a friend. Encourage an exchange of ideas and customs. For example, internationals usually love to show slides of their country. You in turn might introduce them to Christianity. *Always let them know* in advance if there is to be a short talk on Christianity so they do not feel trapped.

These group and individual activities with internationals may stimulate their interest further in smaller group Bible studies led by students, faculty or local Christians on campus or in a home. But remember that personal hospitality is imperative to maintain vital relationships and confidence.

Getting Ready

Preparation for being a genuine friend is a constant process. We *pray* for those we love. We look for practical ways to express our love by *planning* things that are mutually beneficial and interesting to talk about or to do together. *Reading* about a particular student's country, its politics, economics, religion(s), family life and customs can be a highly rewarding part of the relationship. If you can't find anything to read, you can always ask the international to *tell* you about these things.

There are a few basic resources you can use: (1) The library will have a lot of information on a country or religion. (2) In an encyclopedia you can look up any country. Just make sure that printing is up to date! (3) *National Geographic Magazine* has colorful articles on most parts of the world. (4) *Operation World* by P. J. Johnstone (Bromley, Kent, England: Send the Light Publications, 1983) gives brief sketches of every continent and country in the world. It also acts as a prayer guide for world evangelization. Order from the William Carey Library, 1705 N. Sierra Bonita, Pasadena, CA 91104. (5) *A Guide to International Friendship* by Paul E. Little is a seventeen-page booklet from Inter-Varsity Christian Fellowship. It costs 25¢. Order from IVCF, 233 Langdon St., Madison, WI 53703. (6) Check the InterVarsity Press catalog for books related to the world's religions. You can get one free from IVP, Box F, Downers Grove, IL 60515.

Ned Hale is the coordinator of International Student Ministries for Inter-Varsity Christian Fellowship of the U.S.A. This article first appeared in You Can Tell the World, *© 1979 by Inter-Varsity Christian Fellowship of the U.S.A.*

21
Unless They Are Sent

Melvin J. Friesen

The quarterback racing down the field can do so only with the support of a strong offensive line and the assistance of others down the field. Newscasters can highlight the news only because they rely on a large staff of researchers, script writers and technicians. With excited anticipation we watched men on the moon, not being aware or fully recognizing that thousands of planners, engineers, builders, technicians, computer scientists and people posted at lonely tracking stations around the world made these historic steps possible.

It was realizing this sort of thing that likely caused the apostle Paul after stating that "every one who calls upon the name of the Lord will be saved," to continue, "But how are men to call upon him in whom they have not believed? And how are they to believe in him of whom they have never heard? And how are they to hear without a preacher? And how can men preach unless they are sent? As it is written, 'How beautiful are the feet of those who preach good news!' " (Rom. 10:13-15).

Strange how we single out the one who is sent, the missionary, forgetting those who are responsible for sending him or her. How we revel at the moonwalkers, not appreciating the many who made their journey possible; spotlight the newscaster, unaware of the large back-up crew; are oblivious of the team's scramble, focusing on the quarterback with the ball in hand! We have become a nation, a people, of hero worshipers, keying on the performer, paying small attention to those making it possible for the performer to be limelighted.

But let's get back to Paul's series of questions—simple, obvious, but evidently profound. They follow Paul's reminder that Jesus is Lord and that this "same Lord is Lord of all and bestows his riches upon all who call upon him" (Rom. 10:12).

Jesus began his public ministry reading from the scroll of the prophet Isaiah, "The Spirit of the Lord is upon me, because he has anointed me to preach good news to the poor. He has sent me to proclaim release to the captives and recovery of sight to the blind, to set at liberty those who are oppressed, to proclaim the acceptable year of the Lord" (Lk. 4:18-19). This he did! He then issued the call to follow him. He further declared that "As the Father has sent me, even so I send you" (Jn. 20:21). His concluding mandate was to "go into all the world and preach the gospel" (Mk. 16:15).

In proclaiming this good news we take new heart and courage and comfort knowing that Jesus said, "All authority in heaven and on earth has been given to me. Go therefore and make disciples of all nations, baptizing them in the name of the Father and of the Son and of the Holy Spirit, teaching them to observe all that I have commanded you; and lo, I am with you always, to the close of the age" (Mt. 28:18-20). So we see the Lord Jesus who dramatically went so far out of his way to bring us to God through himself calling his followers in unmistakable terms to pass the word along to each succeeding generation to *also* follow him, to be obedient to all that he has commanded them.

Thus he calls us, we who call ourselves by his name. He calls us to go out of our way to bring others to God through Christ Jesus the Lord, proclaiming and demonstrating his redemptive word to the poor, the enslaved, the sick, the oppressed.

Pondering these directives may well leave us in a quandary. If we are to be involved in all that is implied in "going" and also provide back-up for those who do, why does he seem to call us to a reckless abandon of material goods and possessions? "I tell you, do not be anxious about your life, what you shall eat or what you shall drink, nor about your body, what you shall put on. Is not life more than food, and the body more than clothing?" (Mt. 6:25).

Yet on the other hand, in declaring the cost of being a disciple, Jesus uses two illustrations which show how important it is to give meticulous attention to the ingredients necessary for building a tower or for going to battle. "Which of you, desiring to build a tower, does not first sit down and count the cost, whether he has enough to complete it? . . . Or what king, going to encounter another king in war, will not sit down first and take counsel whether he is able with ten thousand to meet him who comes against him with twenty thousand?" (Lk. 14:28, 31).

Jesus is giving us two important principles to note in following him. On the one hand he is telling us what our attitude about things, material possessions, should be. We are not to be anxious or worry about them. He is our provider: he knows about tomorrow. Don't worry about it. We must sow the seed; only he can germinate it.

When he talks about the cost of discipleship, however, and what is really involved in following him, he uses the very down-to-earth, no-nonsense illustration of the planning needed to bring a task to completion.

In the Old Testament the tithe, or tenth, was a requirement of the faithful, to say nothing of additional gifts and extra offerings scheduled periodically. Compassion for all kinds of disadvantaged is implicit and explicit.

In the New Testament one does not hear so much of the tithe although it was a part of the continuing tradition. Rather a greater emphasis is made on the total ownership of our bodies and possessions by God (for example, Rom. 12:1; 14:7-9; 1 Cor. 6:19-20; Rev. 5:9). Our responsibility, then, is one of returning to him what has come into our custody. That is how Jesus' seemingly contradictory principles come together in one. Whether we go or send, it's all under the awareness of his ownership and our desire to do his bidding. If Jesus is Lord (and he is) and I am his (and I am), then it is not a question of whether I will or will not go or send, but how I should be involved in going or sending or both. I am responsible and accountable to God for all that I am and have.

We must stop putting so much emphasis on the "goer" that we forget all that stands behind him or her. We seem obsessed to magnify the last link. There really are no heroes in God's family the way we tend to identify them. Let's exchange the spotlight for the floodlight and notice all of the unheralded steps and people in obscure corners and behind the scenes. If we did this, we would find other notable ones of whom Christ says, "Well done, good and faithful servant!" (Mt. 25:21).

Wherever we are is a mission field. Yet there are always those beyond our reach who are also our responsibility. Those who remain should learn the seriousness of their stay at home and realize that surely the ninety per cent must send the ten per cent. History bears out the fact that many who go were first those who sent. The whole Christian community needs to fast and pray, to experience the joy of knowing that the Holy Spirit is separating some to go and others to send as in the church in Antioch (Acts 13).

So none of us gets off the hook. All are called. Some are called to go. All are called to pray. All are called to give. When the call to commitment is issued, all should step forward, declaring, "Here am I!" So for all of us, then, the question really is: How am I going? or how am I sending? No turning back. No turning back.

Melvin J. Friesen served on staff with Inter-Varsity Christian Fellowship in California until his death in 1983. This article originally appeared in You Can Tell the World, *© 1979 by Inter-Varsity Christian Fellowship of the U.S.A.*

Understanding My Commitment

Throughout this volume on missions you have had an opportunity to pray and think about your own role in God's purposes for the world. Here is a way you can solidify before God what you have learned. Take a few minutes to write answers to these five questions. Try to be as specific as possible.

1. What is my understanding of world mission?

_____

_____

2. What one key thing has God been saying to me about my participation in his world mission?

_____

_____

3. What is my next step in obeying his purpose for me? (Be specific: like getting to know a missionary, writing to him or her, subscribing to a missionary journal, reading a particular book, etc.)

_____

_____

4. In what one thing do I need God's help to activate my next step?

_____

_____

5. Who could I share my commitment with and my need for prayer? His or her name is _____
What day will I do this? _____
Write to the I-V Missions Department for further help: *Inter-Varsity Missions, 233 Langdon, Madison, WI 53703*

POOL to School
Read while you ride

BERKELEY TRiP

644-POOL

We match people
coming & going
your way

READ A BOOK
ON THE
BUS

BERKELEY TRiP

644-POOL

Route • Schedule • Pass Outlet Info.

Questions for Discussion

If we are honest with ourselves about the implications of discipleship, of following Jesus Christ, we must grapple with what Christ says about the world mission of the church. One way to do this is through a group discussion of this book.

The following questions are designed to help a group move through some of the relevant issues. There are eleven studies, seven on the articles in the book and four Bible studies. Each fits comfortably in a 45- to 60-minute time slot. The members of the group should read each article or passage before coming to the discussion.

An outline for using this book with a group might look as follows:

Discussion 1.   Overseas Missions Projects for the 1980s
(pp. 17-19).
Concerts of Prayer: Waking up for a New Missions
Thrust (pp. 20-26).

Discussion 1

Overseas Missions Projections for the 1980s

1. The sheer number of unreached peoples can be overwhelming. Yet with the involvement of every committed Christian, the task can be completed.

In what ways have you already been involved in reaching out to the lost?

What practical things can you or your Christian fellowship begin to do to share Christ's love?

2. What avenues have you already explored in preparation for your role in world missions?

What other practical steps can you take?

Concerts of Prayer
1. How could a reawakening to Christ's lordship "lead ultimately to a new missions thrust?"
2. What does Bryant say is the foundation of an awakening and expansion of Christ's global cause? Why is this so important?
3. Take a close look at the things you pray for. Do you find yourself and/or your group praying mostly for: (a) personal needs and desires? (b) revival? (c) missions?
Explain why you think this has become the major focus of your prayers.
4. Why do you suppose Bryant talks about *b* and *c* above and not *a*?
What are some practical ways to integrate prayer for fullness and fulfillment in *your* life and the life of your fellowship?
5. Look again at Bryant's recommended prayer targets. Choose five areas of prayer from each of the two agendas. Start today to integrate these into your prayer life.

Discussion 2
The Living God Is a Missionary God
1. Why, according to Stott, is it important to know on what grounds the Christian mission rests?
2. What was the context of God's promise to Abraham?
How was the promise of a land, a posterity and a blessing fulfilled in the past?
How is the promise receiving fulfillment in the present?
How will God's promise to Abraham receive its final fulfillment in the future?
3. Looking at Stott's conclusion, what do we learn about God from his promise to Abraham and its fulfillment?
How can knowing these things be motivating as you consider your role in God's plan for the world?
4. Take time to praise God for the things you've learned about him.

The Need in World Mission Today
1. How does Winter define *normal* evangelism?

What is crosscultural evangelism?

2. Explain what is represented by each of the four circles in figure 1 on page 41.

How do you feel about the size of the task remaining?

3. Among the three major blocs, which has the greatest need for evangelism?

What are some of the ways the world differs from the three major blocs?

4. Why do you think most of the energies of the church are focused on those who already consider themselves Christians?

Have you ever attempted to witness to someone outside your cultural sphere?

If so, what was it like?

5. What are some ways the church could attempt to reach more effectively those who do not call themselves Christians?

Discussion 3
The Messenger's Qualifications

1. What is Magalit's response to those who say the day of the Western missionary is coming to an end?

What attitudes does he suggest an American missionary must have today?

2. Briefly describe the three qualifications Magalit says are essential.

What is the scriptural basis of each?

Why is each of these qualities so crucial in missionary work?

3. What can you do to develop each of the qualities mentioned by Magalit?

4. What does partnership in missions mean?

How do some American missionaries thwart partnership?

How can this be avoided?

That Amazing Thing Called the Church

1. MacDonald acknowledges that the church does not always seem relevant to the average student. Has this been your experience? Explain?

2. MacDonald goes on to list six principles that show the church

to be central to God's working in our world. Briefly summarize each of the six principles.
What is the basis for these principles?
3. What can you say about the role of the local church in light of this article?
Does your church fill this role? Explain.
4. What determines the effectiveness of the local church? (See the fifth principle.)
How can you help your church to be more effective in fulfilling its mission? Be specific.
5. Why is it important that you be involved in the church?

World-Class Cities
1. Fifty per cent of the earth's population is urban. How will this fact change the course of evangelization in the future?
2. Discuss Bakke's statement, "God's people should seek to minister not only *in* the city but *to* it as well."
What does he mean by this in his subtitle "Strategies for Evangelism"?
3. What might the worldwide implications be of your reaching out to internationals in your city or on your campus?

Discussions 4 through 7 (See part two, pp. 77-90).

Discussion 8
Before You Go; Once You're There; Hints for Handling an Abnormal Blessing; Talking with Mission Agencies
1. Why would it be a good idea to prepare for Urbana?
What are some of the suggestions Evans-Layng gives for preparing for Urbana?
2. What are some of the draining experiences Treguboff says you could face at Urbana?
3. Which of Hammond's hints would you say is most important? Why?
4. In Shingledecker's and Rutz's article, what factors seem most crucial for you as you investigate various mission agencies?
5. How can attending Urbana be a parable of a missionary ex-

135

perience?
If you are going to Urbana, what steps will you take to get ready
before you go?

Discussion 9
Knowing God's Will
1. How have you applied Munger's suggestions for seeking
God's will?
What has been the result thus far?
What further steps can you take?
2. Specifically, what things might Christ ask you to give up in
order to follow him into a deeper commitment?
3. In what ways are your trusting God to show you his will for
your life?
4. Project ahead forty or fifty years. If you continue on the present course, will you be able to look back over your years and
know that you served God to your fullest capacity? Explain.

The Messenger and Mission Societies
1. Read Acts 13 and 14:24-28. How was the church at Antioch
an early model of a missions sending agency?
Describe the support system offered by the church.
Why were the events of 14:24-28 essential to the ministry of Paul
and his team?
2. What problems do you foresee with tentmaking in a primative
and rural area?
3. What are some of the advantages, according to Webster, of a
missions agency in this kind of setting?

Discussion 10
The Messenger and New Avenues
1. What does Siemens say is the purpose of exploring new avenues in overseas work?
2. Why will traditional means of taking the gospel overseas be
insufficient for completing the task?
3. Evaluate your present skills, field of study and career goals.
How can these be used in any of the new avenues suggested by

Siemens?
4. Discuss the advantages and disadvantages of both mission agencies and tentmaking.

Growing an International Friendship
1. Have you ever known a person from another country well? How did you get to know him or her? How did your friendship grow? What did you learn about yourself in the process?
2. If you have never had a friendship with an international, what fears do you have as you think about forming one?
3. Why do you think internationals respond to the gospel best in the context of friendships with Christians?
4. Which of the suggestions that Hale gives do you think would work best for your fellowship group? Explain.

Discussion 11
Unless They Are Sent
1. Why do people tend to focus on the person in the spotlight rather than on all those who made the achievement possible? How have we tended to do this as Christians?
How does the lordship of Christ challenge such thinking?
2. Friesen mentions two illustrations that Christ gives about handling possessions. What are they? Why do they seem to have opposite conclusions? How are they reconciled into one?
3. What then are the responsibilities of every Christian as regards God's world mission? In which of these responsibilities have you been weak? Explain.

Understanding My Commitment
1. If you have not done so already, take time to answer the questions to Understanding My Commitment (p. 130).
2. Would anyone like to share what they've written? Let's pray for each other's commitments. (Or break up into pairs. Have each take two or three minutes to share what they've written and then another five or ten minutes to pray for each other.)
3. See the World Evangelism Decision Card in the appendix for a possible next step.

Appendix A: *World Evangelism Decision Card*

Through the years God has used the IVCF World Evangelism Decision Card (in various forms, colors and wordings) to confront students with the need to make a personal decision in response to Christ's commission to "go . . . and make disciples of all nations."

During the Urbana convention, you, too, will be given a World Evangelism Decision Card and be asked to consider before God what personal commitment he would have you make to his world mission. This decision card is reproduced here so that you may be familiar with it and be prepared to respond to it when it is presented at Urbana. Copies of the decision card may be obtained by writing: Inter-Varsity Missions, 233 Langdon, Madison, WI 53703.

World Evangelism Decision Card

I acknowledge that:

1. All men without Christ are lost but God in love has given His son that they may have eternal life
2. Jesus Christ is my Lord and Savior and I earnestly desire to recognize His Lordship in every area of my life
3. His command is to go and make disciples of all nations, and I accept that command as my personal responsibility, whether God leads me to go abroad or stay at home

(Check your decision)

☐ **I.** I believe it is God's will for me to serve Him abroad, and I will pray and make inquiry to this end

☐ **II.** Convinced that I have a part in God's plan for the world, I will actively seek His will for me by increasing my awareness of an involvement in world missions.

As a viable indication of my commitment, I will: (select no more than three options)

☐ **A.** Pray daily for specific mission concerns
☐ **B.** Read one or more books about world missions
☐ **C.** Begin a systematic study about world missions
☐ **D.** Join a missions study/action group
☐ **E.** Subscribe to a missions periodical/bulletin
☐ **F.** Develop a friendship with an International student
☐ **G.** Begin to financially and prayerfully support a missionary/national worker
☐ **H.** Make plans to participate in a summer mission program
☐ **I.** Begin corresponding with one or more mission agencies about service opportunities
☐ **J.** Seek further training for preparation to become a missionary

---

My Signature   **Date**

In signing this card, you indicate a desire to discover, and willingness to obey, God's purpose for your life in terms of Christ's commission to "go . . . and make disciples of all nations."

We are pleased to help you in fulfilling your resolve and will send you material designed to assist you. As you correspond with us, we are ready to counsel you personally about openings, mission boards, further preparation and any other specific matters related to your life-work.

Inter-Varsity Christian Fellowship
Student Missions Fellowship
Nurses Christian Fellowship

233 Langdon Street, Madison, WI 53703

745 Mt. Pleasant Road
Toronto, Ontario M4S 2N5

Printed in USA

Appendix B: Mission Services of Inter-Varsity

Inter-Varsity Christian Fellowship is committed to helping students and recent graduates to promote the world mission of the church and to assisting them as they determine their own role in that mission. To achieve this purpose, Inter-Varsity offers the following services to you.

Urbana Onward

A weekend event designed to help recent Urbana participants make application of the things they learned about world missions, in their personal lives and in the life of their chapter or church. Urbana Onward weekends are offered throughout the United States in the few months following each Urbana convention.

Summer Training Programs

Overseas Training Camps—a crosscultural learning and service experience offered each summer in five parts of the world: Latin America, Philippines, Europe, Africa (Kenya and Nigeria) and Asia (Chinese emphasis).

Missions Discipleship Camp—a one-month program combining studies on the world of missions with training in basic discipleship and leadership skills, put in a world dimension. Concludes with an urban crosscultural experience.

Student Training in Missions—includes four weekends of crosscultural communications training from January through April, an eight- to twelve-week summer experience overseas, and a weekend of debriefing in the fall. Applications must be in by November 25.

IVCF also offers a service to help you find specific summer mission programs that fit your own needs and concerns. Write for a form called "So You're Interested in Summer Missions."

Missions Conferences

Urbana Student Missions Convention—this five-day, end-of-December conference is held every three years on the campus of the University of Illinois. The conference brings together thousands of students to participate in a variety of plenary addresses, elective seminars and small group discussions centering on the world mission of the church.

World Christian Video Training Curriculum—demonstrates how the grand sweep of world mission can become a unifying force in your life—as individuals, as small groups, as campus Christian movements and as local churches.

Life with a Purpose—a team of career missionaries are brought together to lead in a weekend of exploration and discussion on crosscultural ministries. Primarily for those serious about investigating such a possibility for their own lives.

Missions Resources

Recommended Reading on the World Mission of the Church—an annotated bibliography on world missions covering: biblical basis, personal preparation, biography, current issues, history, strategy and other topics.

Magazines for World Christians—a listing of some of the best periodicals available, both secular and from mission agencies, to help build your world vision.

Directory of Foreign Mission Agencies—an alphabetical listing of major mission agencies indicating countries in which they work and including addresses and phone numbers of home offices.

In the Gap: What It Means to Be a World Christian—describes what World Christians are, how they think, what they choose and how they take action for Christ's global cause. Includes a wealth of ideas and resources for developing a World Christian lifestyle. Provides the framework for the World Christian booklets. (270 pages, $5.95)

World Christian Booklets—a series of books to help build a world vision, obey the vision and share the vision. Titles include: "World Christian Check-Up," "World Christian Chapter/Church Profile," "Obey the Vision through Prayer," "Magazines for World Christians," "How to Create World Christian Bible Studies," "How to Interview a Real Live Missionary" and "Set World Christian Dreams Free."

Perspectives on the World Christian Movement: A Reader—edited by Ralph Winter and Steve Hawthorne, this collection of articles covers every major area of the modern missionary movement. Subjects include the history of mission, linguistics, world relief, Muslim evangelism, church history, cultural perspectives and mission strategy. We offer this collection at a special reduced price for those interested in IVM materials. (846 pages, $13.00)

World Evangelism Decision Card—used to help students clarify their thinking about and commitment to world missions. Identical to the card used at Urbana. When the second half of the card is returned to Inter-Varsity, appropriate follow-up material is sent free of charge.

Ten Next Steps—a follow-up tool to the World Evangelism Decision Card which details specific resources and ideas to help individuals take action in any of the ten options mentioned on the card. (45¢)

1-800-DECLARE—A toll free number to the Missions Department for those who need some personal counsel in determining that next step. The number is available for missions counseling only, not material orders or Urbana information.

Helps for Your Missions Group

Balanced Missions Emphasis—a paper which describes objectives of a missions emphasis and gives many suggestions for chapter involvement and programs.

IVCF Missions Handbook—a compilation of papers to provide any IVCF chapter with a wealth of information, resources, program ideas and training approaches. ($7.00)

Student Missions Leaders Handbook—a training manual for developing and encouraging missions groups on Christian college campuses—SMF. ($7.00)

Recommended Missionaries/Mission Leaders for a Campus Ministry—a listing of currently available missionaries. Updated annually.

Missions Media

TWENTYONEHUNDRED productions (the multimedia ministry of IVCF) has produced a number of media presentations which provide practical insights into the church's world mission and stimulus for participation in world missions. These presentations are designed for churches, conferences and schools as well as student group meetings, and are available on a rental basis. The media presentations operate only on the Pocket Star 2-projector system: available on an advance-reservation basis from local IVCF staff. For rental details and a brochure describing the media presentations now available, write: TWENTY-ONEHUNDRED, 233 Langdon, Madison, WI 53703.

Overseas Counseling Service (OCS)

An information and counseling service for those seriously considering overseas ministry as a nonprofessional missionary (self-supporting witness). OCS has computerized information on thousands of positions all over the world. Write: Overseas Counseling Service, 1594 N. Allen #23, Pasadena, CA 91104.

For further information about any of these missions services, write: Inter-Varsity Missions, 233 Langdon, Madison, WI 53703.